# Take my Family... Please!

The articles in this book were first published in
*The Toronto Star* and *Star Weekly*
and appear here with the kind permission of
the Toronto Star Syndicate.

*Produced for*
*John Wiley & Sons Canada Limited by:*

**Madison Press Books**
**The Coach House**
**149 Lowther Avenue**
**Toronto, Ontario**
**Canada, M5R   3M5**

**Design:** V. John Lee
**Typesetting:** General Printers
**Printing and Binding:** John Deyell Company
**Cover Photo:** Dick Loek

**A JOHN WILEY & SONS/MADISON PRESS BOOK**

## Canadian Cataloguing in Publication Data

Lautens, Gary.
   Take My Family . . . Please!

Selections from the author's column in the Toronto
Star.

ISBN 0-471-79972-6

1. Lautens family. 2. Family—Anecdotes, facetiae,
satire, etc. I. Johnston, Lynn Franks, 1947-
II. The Toronto Star. III. Title.

PN6231.F3L38      646.7'8'0207      C80-094593-X

# Gary Lautens
# Take my Family... Please!

A JOHN WILEY & SONS/MADISON PRESS BOOK

# *How All This Started Not Even I Am Sure*

I remember taking out this dishy blonde on a first date—it was October 27, 1956, if you are keen on details—and sometime during the evening, either at Maple Leaf Gardens where we saw a hockey game or on the ride home in my cream MG sports car with wire wheels, I looked longingly into said creature's big blue peepers and murmured, "I'd like you to be the mother of my children." Undoubtedly it was something I had heard in an old George Brent movie and, to this very moment, I'm not sure if I was serious.

Probably not.

After all, Jackie was eighteen, I was only a week from my twenty-eighth birthday, and what I was doing, cackle, cackle, was making a pitch, handing out a line, well, let's be frank, softening her up for a little romance, very little if you've ever been in the front seat of a small British sports car with an emergency brake between you and the love object, not to mention enough winter clothing to supply Siberia in a cold snap.

Details aren't important but six months later I have a vague recollection of kneeling together in front of the altar at church and saying "I do" while my bride kept sliding off the satin cushion and giggling, much to the bewilderment of the minister who was already nervous as it was.

Two and a half years later, just in time for Christmas, 1959, we had our first child, a son we named Stephen. Cross my heart, I only assumed we were starting a family, not a cottage industry. I had no intention of using the baby to support me, pay my rent, provide me with luxuries like food and typewriter ribbons; but that is how it worked out.

Although I was writing a sports column at the time, I occasionally broke out in merry paragraphs over our little dish-breaker's latest antic, the cute way he wiggled in his crib, the clever way he mushed his puréed turnip on the kitchen walls and, well, there's no need to go into all of that, especially at this late date. The point I'm struggling to make is that there was no premeditation involved. It just happened.

When Jane came along (June 26, 1962) my news sources doubled and with Richard (October 21, 1964) I had more than enough anecdotes, clever sayings and diaper pail lines to fill a column, so we gave up. A good writer can recognize when he's done enough research.

To bring you up to date, some months ago Jackie decided to go through the 7,000-plus columns I've written over the years, take out the ones about the children, compile a family album for each of them and present them with a chronicle of their growing-up years, whether they wanted it or not. Sometime they might be interested in reading what their father said about them, although to date, they've managed to suppress their curiosity very well. Stephen, Jane and Richard (to answer those who might ask) don't think much of my columns about them for the simple reason they don't read them. They think their father is an arsonist, I suspect, and I see no reason to disappoint them now.

At any rate, having put all the family columns together, we then weeded out all but the ones you see between these covers, thinking that there might be an audience for a book that isn't about dieting, Nazis, a religious cult, how to make a million, Quebec, or how to improve your golf swing in fifteen easy chapters.

So the rest, Dear Reader, is up to you.

Let me merely add that these pieces have appeared in the

*Toronto Daily Star,* the *Panorama* section of the late lamented *Star Weekly,* and the *Toronto Star TV Guide.* The wonderful drawings are by Lynn Johnston who lives with her dentist-husband in Lynn Lake, Manitoba and is regarded as the premier female cartoonist in North America because of her daily comic strip, *For Better or For Worse* and her own best-selling books.

But the leading players in this household drama are Stephen, Jane and Richard Lautens who at 20, 18 and 15 are alive and well in downtown Toronto, and still amusing their father every day. I hope they amuse you, too.

*Gary Lautens*

August, 1980

# *Is There Life After Diaper Pails?*

# What's in a Name?

HAVING A BABY ISN'T ALL CLEAR SAILING. ULTIMATELY
you have to sit down and face facts: Pablum-puss will need a
name.

It's all right to refer to him (or her, since babies come in
two varieties in a democracy) as Precious Secret for a little
while. But you should pick something more solid for the
future.

It's doubtful if the Ottawa Rough Riders would sign a chap
named Precious Secret Jones to a contract. The Argos perhaps—but never the Rough Riders.

So the parents must think to the future. You have to do
something for that lovely baby bonus cheque.

My wife and I have been going over names at a furious
rate, hoping for an inspiration to hit before the Stork.

"According to a poll in the *San Francisco Chronicle,* four out
of seven people like the names they were given," I said the
other evening.

"Shhh!" she replied. "I'm looking at the credits for this
television show."

Yes, that's what she is doing these nights—looking at
screen credits in hopes of discovering a name we both like.
She also reads birth announcements, bread wrappers and
police court news.

"How would you like to give the baby a set of initials and
no name—you know, J. J. Lautens?" she asked.

Apparently there is an assistant casting director named

J. J. Finque, or some such, in Hollywood and my wife was prepared to name the baby after him.

"No," I replied. "I don't know this Finque. Besides, the Fitzsimmons have already used initials. We can't copy them."

"I had forgotten," she admitted.

It's one of the rules of baby-naming that you don't copy anybody else in the entire world. The second rule is that the name must be familiar.

"If it's a girl, how about Lilo?" I suggested.

"Lilo? That's a silly name."

"I like Lilo."

"Is that the name of one of your old girl friends? I bet that's it. Who's this Lilo?"

"But . . ."

"How can you bring up an old girl friend's name when I'm in such a, a, a, delicate condition," she whimpered, throwing a pillow at my head and kicking me in the shins.

I got the impression my wife wasn't in favor of Lilo. She didn't like Casey, Liz, Zizi, Zoe or Rebecca either.

"I like Sarah," she announced.

"Where did you get that name?"

"Never mind. It's simple, homespun, down-to-earth . . ."

It turned out that a lady named Sarah Something-or-other had broken off relations with her breadman in Cape Town, with an axe, according to a news item.

"Sarah is definitely out," I announced. "Besides, the only Sarah I ever knew had thick ankles. I don't want a daughter with thick ankles."

"I like Richard for a boy," my wife continued. "Or Mark."

"We could call him Archbishop—Archbishop Lautens. It would get him a good table at any night club in the country when he grows up," I pointed out.

I could tell by the way my wife dug her fist into my ribs that she didn't like the idea.

"Let's call it off," my wife finally suggested.

"The Baby?"

"No, this discussion about names."

But tomorrow it will start all over again. Have you read any good panel trucks lately?

# Pickles and Ketchup

THE DOCTOR HAD SAID MY WIFE WAS GOING TO HAVE A BABY toward the end of September but thirty days later, and still no baby, we were beginning to get suspicious.

"Maybe he's just kidding us," I said at the breakfast table.

"Pass the pickles," my wife replied.

"How can you eat pickles at a time like this?" I exploded. "Are you sure he said you were pregnant? I just hope this isn't some kind of practical joke."

"Ketchup."

"Ketchup?"

"Yes, ketchup."

"For your pickles?"

"Don't be silly. For my eggs. Who ever heard of putting ketchup on pickles for breakfast?"

"Be serious," I complained. "Maybe it's just your imagination."

"Would you slip on my shoes?" she asked. "I can't bend over my imagination."

"Don't be smart. Why do you want your shoes anyway?"

"Because I think we'll be going to the hospital around noon."

"You mean . . ."

"Yes."

Fortunately, we give our baby business to a hospital that is way behind the times.

You don't have to sit around the delivery room holding

your wife's hand, sharing the rich experience of labor, witnessing the actual birth of a baby.

No. My doctor tells the father-to-be to get lost. He fails to see what good my fainting on the tile floor would be to my wife.

I suppose the nurses could say, "Look at the Jolly Green Giant!" and other amusing things, but he feels that is the wrong kind of encouragement for the mother.

So I always tell them to call me after everything is over. A chap who has to close his eyes when he takes an Alka Seltzer just can't afford to take risks.

But I am very good after the baby is born when everybody is scrubbed and shining. Fairweather friends don't come any more loyal than me.

The test which separates the novices from the seasoned pros (like me) is the nursery room window. That's where you need that extra touch of class.

"Isn't he beautiful?" my wife said as I got my first glimpse of our new son.

"Yes," I replied. "Is the nurse holding him right side up?"

"Of course," she stated.

"I think he looks like your side of the family," I suggested. "Especially when he drools."

However, after studying the other babies in the nursery, I can honestly say we got the pick of the litter. It's remarkable how quality stands out even in one so young.

"Mine's the big fellow over there—the one with the smile and the intelligent look," I mentioned to another father standing by the nursery window.

"Nice," he said, fighting to hide his jealousy. "That's our little guy in the next crib."

"The one with the wrinkled face and all that black hair?"

"He's laughing," he tried to alibi.

"Sure," I agreed.

"How come your boy has waxy hands?" he asked. "Not that I have anything against waxy hands. Some waxy hands are very attractive, especially with that color of skin."

"I can see that waxy hands wouldn't look good with the color of skin your baby has," I admitted. "What color would you call that?"

"What do you mean?"

"Nothing. It's just that it's so mottled. But I'm sure those blotches will go away in time."

"Your son should have very good hearing," he replied. "My! What nice generous ears. Or maybe they just look big because his eyes are so tiny."

"I see they've let your son have a rattle. Oh, I'm sorry. That's his nose, isn't it?" I countered.

"Yours would be quite tall—if he didn't have such bowed legs," my new friend suggested.

And so we bantered back and forth for almost twenty minutes, smiling at each other, he trying desperately to ignore what is as plain as the nose on his child's face—the clear superiority of my son.

I'll be back at the nursery window today, challenging all comers, ready to put our reputation on the line.

Having a perfect baby is quite a responsibility. This is our third. I think a string of successes like that would turn an average man's head. Fortunately, I'm as modest as ever.

# Nothing but the Tooth

WE HAD THE BABY CHRISTENED SUNDAY AT OLIVET Methodist-Presbyterian-Anglican-Congregationalist-Wesleyan-United Church of Canada and things went pretty well. Which means the baby didn't throw up all over my good blue suit during the service.

Nor did the church steeple fall down, a fear the minister had when he spotted my father-in-law in attendance.

The closest we came to an incident was when the minister asked the baby's name. Officially, he's Richard but that's not what we call him around the house.

Our little girl calls him Mr. Nuffin', my other son prefers Porkchops and my wife and I alternate between Peter Perfect and Rotten Kid, depending on the relative humidity of his diapers.

So when the minister asked for a name, I had to do a little thinking and it isn't easy when you're also worrying about a blue suit.

But I came up with it and didn't even break a smile, not even when our baby flashed this big tooth of his to show up the other babies in the church.

I don't like to rub it in when somebody else's kid only has gums. So I felt just awful when the fathers (the ones with the plain children) heard me whisper, "Tell the usher to close the window. The baby's tooth is chattering."

Naturally I apologized and said I could bite my tongue for letting it out and bet our baby felt the same way.

It was cruel the way the church lights just caught his tooth and sort of reflected back on the other parents. I tried to stop him but he put my finger in his mouth and, as I told the other parents, I was surprised he didn't draw blood.

He really crunched. Later, in the church parlor, I pointed out that having a baby with a tooth isn't without its drawbacks, hoping that the others might find some consolation in that.

The other fathers tried to pretend they didn't notice the tooth. One combed his little girl's curl; another tickled his baby's foot to show how he could laugh; two others made a big fuss out of the fact their children were sound asleep and practically toilet-trained.

Some people will do anything to hide a broken heart.

On the way home from church I asked my wife's folks how they liked the service. My father-in-law said it was all right although he didn't recognize the hymns. Any time he's been there in the past, he explained, they always played *Silent Night* or *O Come All Ye Faithful* and *O Little Town of Bethlehem* and he couldn't understand why the minister had got rid of them.

Jackie's mother was too busy to comment. She always is when she's with my children. You see, she has this full-time job of stuffing candies into their mouths.

Apparently she saved all the sweets she wouldn't give Jackie when she was young and now is forced to feed them to her grandchildren so that they won't go to waste.

I would never have found out except that one of my kids begged me not to kill "Granny".

"Why would I kill Granny?" I asked.

He explained that whenever Granny gives him a candy, she warns: "Don't tell your father where you got it. He'll kill me." The rum-and-butter runner is pretty slick.

"What were you thinking about during the service?" I asked my wife who, like me, is very sentimental about such things.

She shifted the baby, a portable crib and the baby linen she was carrying and replied:

"Me? I was thinking—*Stephen! Stop zinging your sister. I was—Jane! Don't eat that candy after it's been on the ground. Or at least brush it off.* It seems that—*Stephen! Didn't I tell you to stop zinging your sister? Now quit it.*"

That baby had a little accident—a moist burp—and my wife had to clean that up before she could finish.

Then the baby pulled off her hat. He would have got her earring, too, but it's the kind that goes right through the ear lobe so he couldn't get it loose no matter how hard he yanked.

"I was just thinking," my wife finally continued, "about how, when we met, you looked at the office where I worked and promised to take me away from all that."

"And I'm as good as my word," I beamed.

"Yes," she said, tears of gratitude and formula running down her cheeks, dress and shoes.


# The Rotten Kid


REMEMBER WHEN YOU WERE YOUNG AND HAD JUST BUSTED something, like your brother, and your mother would look at you and say, "I hope when you grow up you have a child just like you. It will serve you right."

I guess it's the most famous of curses.

Well, it's happened to me. His name is The Rotten Kid.

Outsiders call him Richard but we always say, "Where's The Rotten Kid?"

His sister Jane, who is three, just calls him "Rotten" for short but you know who she means.

The Rotten Kid just turned one and is the reason I look like this a lot of mornings. Last night, for example, we caught him eating the dog's dinner.

Now that may not seem unusual but the dog weighs 195 pounds and The Rotten Kid weighs twenty-three pounds, soaking wet, of course.

Most people are a little timid about taking food from the mouth of a cranky, 195-pound dog but The Rotten Kid isn't impressed by long teeth and bad breath. He wades in anyway, figuring the dog should learn to share.

The other day we left him alone for about eleven seconds, came back into the kitchen and found him standing on top of a glass table, gnawing on a candle.

I know. The child psychologists will say The Rotten Kid needs more love, that he really feels hungry for affection and is eating my candles as a substitute.

I would give him all sorts of love and affection. I swear I would. But The Rotten Kid never stays in one spot long enough for me to deliver.

The other kids were normal enough about walking. Stephen walked at his first birthday, Jane at thirteen months. But The Rotten Kid was walking at ten months.

He had learned to fall down the front porch steps by eleven months, a clear edge of eight months over his brother and sister.

And he was just as precocious on the cellar stairs although he hasn't quite learned how to make a non-stop fall since the side-door landing still interrupts his trip.

My father-in-law had a birthday recently and everybody said how young he looked. They especially admired his color, the glow of his cheeks.

Actually, he can thank The Rotten Kid.

Whenever my wife's father comes for a visit, The Rotten Kid rushes to the door and spends the next hour swinging from the end of his grandfather's tie.

He likes that almost as much as stuffing towels down the toilet.

In any case my father-in-law has come to be known as a man with rosy cheeks and long ties.

We have to close off the rooms in the house because The Rotten Kid can get into trouble wherever he is. For example, he likes to go through his mother's things and trail them through the house.

You can't very well entertain and keep your composure when a little kid walks through the living room, swinging a brassiere over his head, my wife has discovered.

We lose more tradesmen that way.

No, The Rotten Kid is an absolute terror. He eats crayons, knocks over tables, flips his cereal on the walls, bites anyone he can reach on the nose, hollers unless you share your dinner with him, climbs up the furniture so he can swing on lamps, pictures and drapes.

And when he goes to bed at night he has enough energy left for one last kick, surrendering to his sleepers only after a final, monumental battle.

Then he gives you a big smile, tucks the corner of his blue blanket in his mouth and falls asleep.

In his crib he looks like a tiny angel. And, between you and me, that's what I think he is.

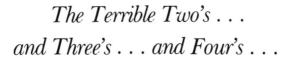

*The Terrible Two's . . .*
*and Three's . . . and Four's . . .*

# Don't Blame Me

FOR YEARS THE EXPERTS HAVE TOLD US THAT BEHIND EVERY rotten kid there is a rotten mother. And, like everybody else, I accepted that.

However, a new school of thought is developing which suggests that maybe fathers have something to do with the behavior of youngsters, too.

Obviously I can't let a charge like that go unanswered. I'd like to say a few words in my defence.

For example, when the television repairman was at our house the other day, up to his shoulders in tubes, transistors and trouble, I did not instruct my five-year-old son to say, "Do you know what you're doing, mister?"

That was his own idea. Or, perhaps, his mother's. But not mine. I never talk that way until after the bill is made out.

And then there was the incident at the restaurant when I had the family out *en masse*, scrubbed, polished and on their best behavior.

We were all seated at the table except for my oldest child (who was in the washroom), when a radio executive came over to meet my wife.

It was very pleasant and proper until he asked my three-year-old daughter, "And who's missing from the table, honey?"

"My brother, the skunk," she said.

I think you know me well enough to realize I don't teach

children to talk like that. I don't teach them to fight either but that's what they do constantly.

Just last evening they were at it again, grabbing, poking, pinching.

Apparently their fists got tired because Jane, who is three, finally suggested, "Let's not fight any more. Let's play house."

Stephen thought about it and then replied, "Okay. And, Jane, let's pretend we like each other."

I don't see how the experts can blame me for that.

The next thing you know they'll be saying it's all my fault that Stephen gave his mother a big hug, patted her blouse and said, "Gee, you're lumpy, Mom."

Nor have I encouraged the baby to retrieve diapers from the pail and drag them across the living room floor as a present for our company.

And the way he screws up his nose when he hands over the gift is his idea, too.

Consider their eating habits.

They don't have any because they never eat, not the two oldest ones.

In fact, when I gloated the other day that neither of them has had a cavity yet, my wife replied, "Why should they? They never use their teeth—except to bite each other."

Certainly that's not my fault. I eat until I see the little bear's face at the bottom of my dish and it's been years since I bit anything that might bite back.

No, the experts are wrong. This father is clean.

I don't throw lamb dinner on the walls. I don't bounce on chesterfields. I don't sneak into the cupboards and throw pots and pans all over the floor. I don't try to catch the goldfish in my hand. I don't suck marking pencils. I don't walk around trying to stick my finger in my brother's nose.

(And on the way to nursery school I don't try to wind up the car window with somebody's head sticking outside.)

Those are things they picked up on their own or, possibly,

from their mother while I've been at work. I would never treat me the way they do.

# Hanging Around

IT'S GETTING MORE AND MORE FASHIONABLE TO HANG *objets d'art* in your home. And no wonder.

A beautiful painting brings an enrichment to the soul. A lovely sculpture communicates great feeling without a word. Art stirs the emotions and gives expression to the torment and joy of the human spirit.

It also bugs the neighbors.

Most collectors specialize in a particular period or school or style. However, I prefer to concentrate on a particular color—green.

It should be on the face of your best friend when he spots your latest acquisition if you are to feel the kind of satisfaction that real art can bring.

Unfortunately, art collecting is an expensive hobby, and, if you are like me (cheap), you try to find a loophole.

We had a bare spot on a front room wall which just cried out for a bit of color—you could hear the sobs on a still night halfway to the corner—but, after looking at prices, I decided it would be better to have a broken-hearted wall than a broken-hearted me.

That's when I came up with a brilliant idea.

I dug out a self-portrait my son did when he was four, a wild thing executed by the artist with several well-placed thrusts of his pointed brush into the vital organs of some yellow construction paper.

It consists of black circles, maroon blobs and patches of blue and red paint.

I can still hear the artist when he presented it to me and I stood, mouth agape, spellbound by its beauty.

"You're holding it upside-down, Daddy," he complained.

Anyway, I purchased an expensive wooden frame, making certain the artist's signature—a simple but sincere "S"—was clearly visible, and hung the painting in plain view.

Frankly, it's worked like a charm.

People who visit are immediately attracted to it and feel obliged to make some comment, usually generous, often extravagant.

"I do like the brushwork," one neighbor admitted. "Imaginative, full of excitement and probably awfully expensive."

I just smiled, delighted that I had finally evened the score for that swimming pool she put in her backyard last summer.

"Who is the artist?" she asked, levelling a cold stare at her husband and his cheque book.

"That's my secret," I said. "Once the word gets out I'm afraid his prices will skyrocket. So I'm keeping him to myself a little while longer."

"A hint wouldn't hurt surely."

"Let me just say he's young, Canadian and very promising."

I like to think I ruined her day. It was marvellous.

When the family doctor stopped in after making his rounds (in the low eighties, he said), even he was impressed. "Now that's what I call a painting," he admitted.

Others have called it "bold" and "primitive" and "daring in concept." The "freedom of expression" was commented upon six times and two men took me aside and asked: "How do you get away with it? My wife would never let me put anything as risqué as that on the walls. Wowee!"

The closest we got to criticism was when the milkman stopped by for his money and said he wasn't sure if he liked modern art. "But that one kinda grows on you, doesn't it?" he qualified.

However, I made one mistake. I invited my neighbor to make a comment.

"It looks like something a kid would do," he stated simply.

Can you imagine that? I have a notion not to invite him back next week when we have an unveiling of the artist's latest self-portrait, done in his mother's lipstick and mascara.


# Dig Those Bones

THE OTHER MORNING MY SON ANNOUNCED THAT HE WOULD like to go to the museum and see dinosaur bones and some of the other items which his kindergarten teacher told him were on display.

"Why don't you turn on the television and watch cartoons," I suggested. "Popeye's Playhouse is on now."

"I don't like Popeye," he whined. "I want to go to the museum."

"It's too cold," I said, rattling my newspaper and sinking a little deeper into my easy chair.

"I'll wear my pyjamas under my pants," he offered.

"They don't have a TV at the museum," I warned.

"I don't like TV," he stated sullenly.

"You can even watch one of those shows which gives you nightmares," I bargained, figuring he could never resist that bit of cheese.

"I want to go to the museum," he replied.

"Why don't you wrestle your sister or crayon on the walls like any normal five-year-old kid?" I wanted to know.

"I'm going to tell my teacher you wouldn't take me to the museum," he threatened.

That was the clincher. On a Saturday morning when it's cold and windy the last thing I need is a museum. But I'm not going to take the chance of getting a bad reputation with any kindergarten teacher.

"Let's stop for something to warm us up," I suggested as we walked into the museum. "They have a swell coffee shop in the basement. You can have . . ."

"I want to see all the guns and swords," he reported, heading straight ahead.

I trailed along as he marched from one exhibit to another.

"This one has eight barrels," he would say. Or, "Did they use swords when you were young, Daddy?"

"These exhibits are all pretty much the same," I pointed out. "I think we can skip the rest of . . ."

"No. I want to see them all," he insisted.

So we trooped from one aisle to another until I suggested that, perhaps, I could wait for him at the door.

"I need you to read to me," he stated scuttling that plan.

"Don't you have to go to the bathroom?" I asked after we had knocked off a couple of rooms and about ten million exhibits.

"No," he said. "What's up the stairs?"

I told him it was mostly a storage area and not worth looking at. However, he wanted to see for himself.

"You're wrong, Daddy," he said joyfully as he hit the second floor and spotted some dinosaur bones fastened together with wire.

"They must have changed things," I grumbled.

We walked through that wing of the building and saw some stuffed animals and paraded past an array of fish and snakes and then paused at the stairway where I had to hold him out over the railing so he could see the top and bottom of the totem pole.

"I'll bet you could use a nice, cold drink and a piece of chocolate cake," I tempted.

"Let's go up to the next floor," he answered.

So we saw Chinese exhibits, Greek exhibits, Egyptian exhibits and young school children giggling at the statues.

The best thing I saw was the elevator which, however, we didn't use.

"We had better sit down," I said. "I don't want to tire you out. Your mother might get mad at me."

"I'm not tired," he unfortunately revealed.

However, I finally convinced him he should stop for something to eat so that he wouldn't wind up looking like that mummy he stared at so intently in the wooden box.

"Let's take the stairs down to the cafeteria," he suggested. "We can race."

During lunch he said he would like to hurry because there was plenty of museum we hadn't seen yet—like the Indian stuff in the basement.

That's when I put my foot down.

"We're going to go to the show this afternoon and see a Disney movie whether you like it or not. And we're going to sit through the whole thing," I instructed.

So that explains why that little boy I was pulling by the hand out of the museum was crying. I just hope he doesn't blab to his kindergarten teacher.

# One Christmas Card Coming Up

EVERY YEAR IN DECEMBER WE GO THROUGH WHAT IS KNOWN as Picture Time at our house. It's sort of like World War Three but without rules.

The tradition started years ago when my wife and I thought it would be a good idea to have a Christmas card featuring our children and dog. It would be folksy, we agreed. And, since we didn't intend to be explicit about the children's faith, nobody could take religious offence.

However, there was one problem: we didn't have any children or dog.

I was all for renting but my wife figured it would be cheaper in the long run to have our own.

So I wound up having these three kids and a St. Bernard dog (my wife can do anything if she puts her mind to it) on my hands.

For 364 days in the year they cost me money but on the 365th they have their one duty to perform: they pose for our Christmas card.

Well, yesterday was it.

For some unknown reason we never get the same photographer twice. In fact, last year the one we had never even came back for his hat.

All we want is a simple picture of three sweet kids and a lovable 195-pound dog smiling in the Christmas spirit.

I can't think of anything easier than that.

But it never quite works out that way.

I assembled the cast and converged on the rec room only to find the floor littered with laundry.

"What are the sheets doing all over the bar stools?" I asked.

"They're supposed to be there," my wife replied.

"Why?"

"To look like snow," my wife explained. "Could you tell they're bar stools covered with sheets?"

"Never in a million years," I said. "It looks exactly like snow."

"Should we put the children on a toboggan and have it pulled by the dog?" my wife asked. "I could bend a coathanger and make it look like a pair of antlers."

"Sounds swell," I encouraged.

"You don't think it looks a little phony, do you?" she wanted to know.

"Don't be silly. I would never guess that it's a dog pulling a toboggan across a rec room floor past some bar stools covered with white sheets," I said. "If I didn't know better, I'd swear I was looking in on a scene in the Laurentians."

My wife seemed pleased with that.

"Stephen!" she ordered. "Stop crossing your eyes." And then she added to me, "Do you think we should dress them like elves?"

I said it was fine by me. "Everything's fine, just as long as we hurry."

The photographer, meanwhile, was setting up his lights and trying to keep out of reach of the dog who was going around smelling everybody's breath to see what they had enjoyed for dinner.

"Didn't you give the dog a tranquilizer?" I asked.

"No, I thought you had," my wife said.

"He's just a little excited," I explained to the photographer who was trying to get his camera bag out of the dog's mouth without much success. "C'mon, boy. Give us the bag."

"Jane! Stop punching your brother," my wife interrupted. You'll make him blink for the picture."

We finally got the camera bag and the kids took their place and our "reindeer" gave a big yawn.

"Smile!" the photographer pleaded.

I made faces.

My wife waved toys.

It was swell except that nothing happened. One of the elves had pulled the floodlight cord out of the wall socket and was trying to screw it into his sister's ear.

There's no point going into all of the details. Within ninety minutes, or so, we had our picture and the photographer gratefully retrieved his camera bag and left. Next year I think I'll handle it differently.

I'll mail out the kids and the dog directly and not bother with a photograph.

# Grime and Punishment

I AM AFRAID I HAVEN'T KEPT UP WITH THE EATING HABITS
of children and am a poorer father as a result.

Let me explain.

The other day I got home from work to be greeted by my
wife at the front door. She was mad. I could tell by the way
she tapped her fingers nervously on the baseball bat in her
hand.

"Well, do something," she said. "They're your children."

"Hi, there," I replied.

"Which one do you want to punish first?"

"Nice day," I persisted. And then I grabbed her hand and
kissed it, right smack on top of her white knuckles.

Well, charm didn't work; obviously I was going to be
required to listen to the whole sordid story.

It seems that my young son, Stephen, had spent most of
the day picking flowers, lovely tulips, to be specific.

"That's nice," I said.

"They were in someone else's garden," my wife added.
"He had picked twenty-eight of them before he was caught."

I made a note of that on the dossier.

"And your daughter! Well, I've never been so embarrassed
in my life."

Let me quickly sketch in the details.

The assistant minister of the church, a kindly old gentle-
man, dropped by the house to see if we've changed much
since Christmas. I think our smiling envelope has been
missed.

Before leaving, he said he would like to give a little prayer.
Heads were bowed and it was appropriately silent—until the

little girl shouted out the only word she knows to indicate a visit to the bathroom would be in order.

And she persisted. So did he.

I think it was about the time he was blessing the people who held the church mortgage that my wife peeked.

Jane was standing in the middle of the living room with her leotards at her ankles. It sort of broke up the meeting.

I summoned the culprits.

"Okay, just for that no candy tonight," I decreed.

"Hurrah," said the children.

"Didn't you hear me? No candy, I said."

They clapped their hands and came over and gave me a hug.

"We hate candy," Stephen said.

My wife kicked my ankle and said I had played right into their hands. "The candy drops are really vitamins," she whispered. "I make them take them every night before they go to bed."

Obviously I had to try something else and was pretty baffled until it struck me that, as a boy, the worst punishment of all was to be sent to bed with only porridge for supper.

"And for supper tonight you can only have cereal," I stated firmly.

"What a good daddy!" Stephen exclaimed, hopping up on my knee and giving me a kiss.

Jane jumped up and down to show her happy reaction to the sentence.

My wife cleared her throat and I knew right away I was in trouble.

"I want that new cereal with the marshmallow bits in it," Stephen suggested. "Or else the fruit flakes."

"But . . ."

The female convict had fled to the kitchen meanwhile and come back with carmel-flavored puffs which, so I learned later, are made especially for little girls.

By then Stephen had second thoughts. He liked the raisins

(although not the bran) in one variety and said there was much to commend the cereal which has been "shot, through and through" with sugar.

They both liked another type, the one that comes with peanuts, but finally decided on something that tastes exactly like a malted milk shake, "only crunchy."

I think that was the one with the storybook package. Or did it have punch-out pictures of the farm animals on the back? It doesn't matter.

"I only give them cereal as a reward," my wife said without moving her lips.

But by now the children had the cocoa flakes and were out on the front lawn, showing the other kids who were filled with envy and begging for a taste.

"And we don't have to eat any candy," I heard Stephen shout to his host of friends.

I think they were all heading up the street to pick tulips when I saw them last.

# Getting the Bird

THE TURKEY WAS IN THE MIDDLE OF THE DINNER TABLE, stuffed, steaming and roasted to a beer brown.

"Boy oh boy!" I said. "Hand me the knife. I'll carve."

"What is it?" my son Stephen, who is six, asked.

"A turkey."

"I don't want any," he said.

"Sure you do. It's good. Try some white meat."

"No. I don't want any turkey."

"Aren't you feeling well?"

"I feel fine but I don't want any turkey."

"Okay," I said, cutting off some slices for other members of the family, saving the hip for myself, of course.

"Dad?" said Stephen as I reached inside for a spoonful of dressing.

"Yes."

"That turkey was alive, wasn't it?"

"Why, I guess so," I answered.

"How did it die?"

"I don't know," I admitted.

"Did somebody kill it?"

"If you don't want to eat, leave the table," his mother said. And then she added, "I don't think I'll have any dressing tonight."

"But Dad, why did they kill the turkey?" Stephen insisted.

"Maybe it just dropped dead," I said.

"Dad, the turkey didn't drop dead, did it? Somebody killed it."

"Maybe," I replied.

"How did they kill it?"

"Let's talk about it later," I suggested, trying to think of some way I could get around that child psychology book which claims you should always be honest with children.

"Dad, isn't it cruel to kill things, especially animals?"

I just smiled, putting some of the turkey and dressing back on the platter. "I'm not as hungry as I thought," I explained.

And then, with great dramatic flair, Stephen proceeded to explain his version of how the turkey was rubbed out.

"The farmer took off his feathers and chopped off his head with an axe," Stephen stated.

His three-year-old sister, Jane, loved the story.

"Why didn't you tell him that turkeys grow on trees, like apples?" my wife complained.

"It wouldn't be honest," I said. "At six he's just sensitive about these things."

My wife and I decided to skip the turkey and go right to

dessert. Nobody had much appetite anyway, except Jane.

"What's for dessert?" Stephen asked.

"Rice pudding," my wife said.

"I don't want any."

"What's wrong with rice?" I asked. "It isn't an animal. Nobody killed the rice or chopped off its head."

"I know," Stephen said. "But I had a sandwich over at Greg's before dinner and I'm not hungry."

And then he left the table.

DAD... HOW DID THE
TURKEY DIE?

# Show and Tell

I HATE TO BE THE ONE TO SQUEAL BUT SCHOOL HAS TURNED my son into a liar.

It's true.

For seven years Stephen was a regular little George Washington. Sodium Pentathol ran in his veins.

We didn't have to worry about a credibility gap.

Stephen would always come clean.

Now that's all changed.

Stephen has discovered that truth doesn't pay—not at Show and Tell Time in Grade Two.

The trouble started a few weeks ago because I appeared on a television show.

Stephen felt he should release the news to his classmates at Show and Tell.

However, I could tell by his face when he got home at four o'clock that it had been a flop.

"They wouldn't believe me," he said simply.

And he went into his room and played quietly until supper.

He didn't even have the heart to wrestle his brother or choke his sister that night. He was deeply hurt.

A couple of days later Stephen decided to make a comeback at Show and Tell.

"I'm going to tell the kids about Geordie," he announced at breakfast. "I bet nobody else has a dog that weighs 200 pounds."

He went off to school, skipping and whistling.

Well, you've guessed it.

Stephen told the kids about his dog; he explained how his dog sleeps outside even when it's ten degrees below zero. And he concluded by saying his dog is practically big enough to ride.

The kids just hooted.

They accused Stephen of making up the entire story and nothing he could say would change their minds.

"Could I take Geordie to school and show them?" he

begged that night. "Then they'd have to believe me."

We told him he couldn't.

About that same time Stephen brought home a report card and it commented on his "wonderful imagination."

Then came the final, crashing blow.

A friend of ours is an amateur taxidermist and he brought out his latest specimen to show us—a tropical fish that must be five feet long.

Stephen couldn't wait to tell the kids at Show and Tell.

I didn't even ask Stephen about their reaction that evening. One look was enough to tell me it was a disaster.

Yesterday was Show and Tell Time again and Stephen was trying to determine what to use as his contribution.

"Why don't you tell them about my cousin, Morris, and how he's a fur trader up north with the Ekimos?" I suggested.

Stephen shook his head.

"I think I'll tell them I had a nosebleed," Stephen interrupted.

"But you haven't had a nosebleed," I said.

"I know," Stephen replied. "But I think they'd believe that."

# Fly Now—Zip Later

WE HAVE WALL-TO-WALL KIDS AT OUR PLACE. OURS AND somebody else's. I'm either living in a nursery or in a home for midget wrestlers. But I wouldn't have it any other way.

It's not exactly that I'm a Father Goose who enjoys being accosted by tiny sheriffs popping up from behind the chesterfield and announcing, "Bang! I gotcha!"

But where else can you get so many laughs for a peanut butter sandwich and bathroom privileges?

Take my six-year-old son Stephen's crowd.

First of all there's Donald. Now Donald looks as if he should be a butcher when he grows up. He's plump, rosy-cheeked, never without a smile.

And he's never zipped up.

I have seen him perhaps a thousand times and I have never yet seen him with his trousers done up.

When you greet Donald, you say: "Hello, Donald, zip up."

He says, "Oops. Hello, Mr. Lautens."

The other day he knocked on our door, calling for Stephen. There he stood, plump, rosy-cheeked, smiling and unzipped. The only difference was he had a paper mask over his eyes.

"Hello, Donald," I said. "Zip up."

"How did you know it was me?" he asked, genuinely shocked. "I'm wearing my Batman mask."

"It was just a guess," I suggested.

Not long ago Donald asked me if I ever saw his mother in church.

"No," I admitted. "I don't."

"I didn't think you would," he answered. "She goes to the Catholic church."

In the same crowd is another grade-one student named Art. A few days ago his mother was going to the store and wanted Art to come along.

"I don't want to," he complained. "And I don't want you to go either."

His mother argued for a few minutes and then decided that Art could stay in the apartment while she and Art's small sister walked over to the store.

Simple, right? That's what Art's mother thought.

She got back about twenty minutes later, opened the apartment door and was confronted by a burly policeman.

Art's mother was slightly shaken. Was there a fire? An accident? Had something gone wrong?

"The boy telephoned the police station," the officer explained, "and told us his mother had run away and left him."

The look was pretty accusing.

Art's mother tried to explain, finally satisfied the constable—and all the time Art stood there, smiling innocently.

My own children (The Rotten Kid and his older brother and sister who are sometimes referred to as Frank and Jesse) got up before we did the other Sunday morning.

When we arrived in the kitchen there was an empty cake box on the table.

"We took a vote and decided to have cake for breakfast," Stephen announced. From what I could gather, the vote was 3-0 although it's difficult to get anything out of The Rotten Kid who only says, "da-da-dada" and an occasional, "tickle-tickle."

Stephen and his three-year-old sister have bunk beds and were talking and arguing (that's what they do best) when I overheard them a few evenings ago.

"I'm not going to marry you when I grow up," Jane threatened.

"And I'm not going to marry you," Stephen replied. "I'm going to marry my mother."

"You can't," Jane stated.

"Why not?" Stephen asked.

"Because she'll be dead," Jane replied.

I'd tell you more but my group took the snow shovel out before the big blizzard and left it lying somewhere in the backyard although nobody remembers exactly where.

So I'm still looking.

Have you ever tried to find a shovel buried under a snow drift sixty feet wide, fifty feet long and up to your ascot deep?

Yes, I owe a lot to my kids but, if I wear a hat, it'll never show.

# One-up-boy-ship

DOCTOR, IT'S THOSE HEADACHES AGAIN. THEY'VE COME back. I can't face people any more and I have this hopeless inferiority complex.

What? Lie down? Of course, Doctor.

Doctor, I've never been hyper-sensitive. I mean, I didn't take it personally when automatic elevators let me off at the wrong floor or when soft drink machines rejected my coin.

But now I know the truth. Doctor, I'm inadequate. I've failed as a parent and everybody knows it.

Max, at the office, tells me his kids are learning Russian and do the crossword puzzles in *The Times* and have been accepted for advanced ballet.

And the oldest it just seven.

Charlie informed me just the other day that his son won three ribbons at the school field day, has just finished building a working model of the *Polaris* and plays the violin.

I hate to say this, Doctor, but I'm the only man in the world with dumb kids.

My kids speak only one language—and we haven't been able to figure out which one that is because they always have their mouths full.

We're not even sure the youngest can talk because he always goes around the house with a blanket in his mouth.

The only trick he knows is how to put raisins up his nose.

But he can't speed-read, scuba dive, make out an income-tax form or drive the family car.

And he's already past two.

I know, Doctor, you're going to say he'll outgrow it. But his sister is four and all she does is watch television, pinch her brother and steal her mother's perfume.

Oh, I thought I had met somebody with a kid as ordinary as mine. But it was a false alarm.

Bill and I were talking about children and he admitted to me that his kid was "just average."

Naturally, I was delighted. Thank God there's another kid in the world who doesn't understand Einstein's theory or can't quote Ovid in the original Latin or doesn't build hi-fi systems in his spare time, I said to myself.

"Yes, my kid's just average," Bill repeated, "average—among the gifted, of course."

Pow! My bubble burst.

So my oldest kid is seven and all he does is bring home fish in a pail and want to keep them in the bath or put his pyjamas on over his clothes so he doesn't have to dress in the morning.

And what he does in his spare time is throw mudballs at frogs.

He doesn't skip grades, paint in oils, read German science texts, do brain surgery, fix carburetors or captain his Little

League baseball team. In fact, he isn't on any team.

What's that, Doctor? You want to show me a photograph of your son? You say he's only five and Harvard has offered him a scholarship and the Yankees consider him a sure-fire major league pitcher and . . . Help! Help!

# Till Kids Do Us Part

OUR HOUSE WAS FILLED WITH MURDERERS AGAIN LAST night. That's the fourth time this month.

We've also had three attacks by savage Indians, an invasion from outer space and twelve curtains that made threatening gestures.

And, if you don't believe me, ask my children.

It was the seven-year-old's turn last night to discover the bloodthirsty plot to wipe out the family.

He woke me up at three a.m. to report, "Somebody's hiding in my closet. Can I sleep with you?"

"There's nobody in your closet," I told him.

"Yes there is. I heard him," he insisted.

"Go back to bed," I reasoned.

"What's wrong?" my wife interrupted.

"Somebody's hiding in my closet," my son explained.

"He's having another one of those dreams," I said.

Well, before I knew what hit me (it was a sharp elbow and a bony knee) there were three of us in bed.

And I was the one on the outside, the one with the bare overhang.

But of course, Dear Parent, you know what I'm talking about.

It's not what you had in mind when you cornered that lovely, shy girl after the basketball game and asked her to be your wife.

You got married so that the two of you could be alone.

Ninny!

Husbands are never alone with their wives. The children won't stand for it.

Have you ever tried to sneak a kiss from your wife before you go to work in the morning? More important, have you ever succeeded?

Of course not.

Just as you go into the embrace, something comes between you—something named Leonard who has a runny nose and wants a drink and steps on your toes.

Surely you don't think that's an accident?

No, it's part of a vast international plot by children to make sure adults are never left alone.

Try to talk to your wife quietly. Make a date to meet her in the basement behind the furnace. Tell her you'll knock on the cold air return three times and that you'll wear a carnation in your buttonhole so she can recognize you.

Schedule your rendezvous for midnight. Schedule it for the Gobi Desert if you want. It doesn't matter.

The children will beat you to the punch.

They will be there first, asking for piggyback rides, wanting you to read them a story, begging for the loan of a kitchen knife so they can carve their initials in the family dog.

They come at you in shifts.

That's why they invented the nightmare (in 1923)—so that they can watch you 'round the clock. Then they came up with the ultimate weapon—the quivering lower lip.

Now, besides never being alone with your wife, you don't get any sleep either.

Why are children doing these things?

Simple. They plan to take over the world. By gradually destroying adults, bit by bit, they feel they can be in charge by 1995 without firing a shot.

# Birthday Competition

WE'VE BEEN WORRYING ABOUT MY DAUGHTER'S BIRTHDAY party for weeks. After all, it isn't every day a girl turns five.

However, as I discovered, a birthday party isn't just a party in the suburbs.

It's a happening. It's an occasion. But, mostly, it's a status symbol.

"I think we should go over the menu for the party," my wife said to me about a month ago.

"What menu?" I replied. "You serve wienies and chocolate milk. Who needs a menu?"

"Do you want us to be the laughing stock of the neighborhood?" she asked in horror. "You can't serve wienies and chocolate milk at a birthday party."

"The Fitzsimmons had a caterer for Carrie's birthday," my wife reminded me. "We can't let them get away with that."

"I was thinking of sirloin roasts, an assortment of salads and an ice cream cake carved into the shape of a little girl—life-sized. We can do it for about ten dollars a guest, counting help. That's about $400."

"Four hundred dollars?"

"Yes. Now for the entertainment. The Johnsons hired a magician for Donald's party. The Turliuks took the kids on a hay ride and the Ruddys had the bowling party, remember?

"I think a theatre party would be nice. You could get

thirty-five orchestra tickets—better make that forty just to be sure—and the closer to the stage the better."

"Are you out of your mind?" I asked. "This party will cost $1,000."

"Just $600," my wife answered. "Matinee tickets will be fine."

"Those kids will eat wienies and drink chocolate milk and play pin-the-tail-on-the-donkey," I blurted. "And I'll give you two dollars in dimes to put in the cake. But that's it."

Then my conscience began to work on me. Some time ago we were at a house party and my wife volunteered to be a subject for a minister who dabbled in hypnosis.

To show what the subconscious can recall, he asked my wife various questions, including one about her own fifth birthday.

She began to cry.

Later we learned that my wife had never had a fifth birthday party because it was wartime and her father was away in the Navy.

Naturally, I didn't want that to happen to my daughter.

"Okay," I shouted through the bedroom door. "I'll give you seventy-five bucks to put on the birthday party."

That seemed to soothe my wife some.

However, yesterday I got a call at the office.

"The birthday party's off," my wife said, obviously fighting back the tears.

"Why?" I asked.

"Jane's got chicken pox," she replied.

# Debbie, the Babysitter

I'D BE SUNK IF ANYTHING HAPPENED TO DEBBIE.

Debbie is our babysitter and that makes her about the most important person in my life.

I can't make a move without her and she knows it. If I want to go to the show or the ballgame or the ballet or even to a house party, I have to ask Debbie's permission first.

If she agrees. I go. If she says no, I'm as immobile as a statue on a postcard.

Sometimes it's confusing to the people who invite me out.

"Yes, a barbecue sounds like fun," I tell them, "but I'd better check with Debbie to see if we're free that night."

They immediately think I must have a girl friend because they know my wife's name is Jackie.

But there's no point calling Jackie. I know she'll go anywhere, provided the kids don't come and she doesn't have to do dishes.

The key is Debbie.

Every Monday night my wife telephones Debbie to make our booking and it turns into a three-way conversation.

"Debbie wants to know what night we want her," my wife asks.

"Saturday," I suggest.

My wife relays the message and then turns to me again. "Debbie says Saturday is out of the question this week. She's got a date."

"How about Friday?" I ask.

"Debbie says Friday may be all right," my wife reveals, holding her hand over the mouthpiece of the phone. "She wants to know where we're going."

"Just to a movie or something," I answer.

"Debbie wants to know if we'll be late," my wife asks next.

"I don't think so," I tell her.

"Can we be home by midnight?" my wife wants to know.

"Yes."

"Good." The it's all right with Debbie. She has to get up early Saturday morning and she doesn't want to be late."

Gratefully, we await Debbie's arrival on Friday night.

We put on the TV for her. We tell her there's grape soda (her favorite) in the refrigerator. We show her the new ma-azines. And we promise to telephone to see if the kids are behaving.

Why not?

She is only fifteen or sixteen, slender as a blade of grass and terrifically shy. But she looks like Sophia Loren, Venus de Milo and Joan of Arc when she comes through the front door.

Sometimes she even lets us out of the house two or three times in the same week. Just last month she gave us permission to stay at a party until almost 1:30.

Alas! Debbie is on holidays right now. She doesn't get home until the 3:09 train Sunday afternoon.

And we can't even get to the corner unless we take all three kids with us, including Richard who is the rotten one.

We're all going nuts—my wife, my kids and me.

It seems as if we've got a terminal case of togetherness. My wife has missed a sale of material. I can't see that movie downtown I've been waiting for. The kids are tired of going to bed without grape soda.

So hurry home, Debbie.

We love you.

# Rent-A-Kid

A LOT OF PEOPLE ARE GETTING MARRIED AT THIS TIME OF year—the autumn wedding is lovely with the leaves turning brown and the groom turning green.

And these young couples are usually undecided about one thing: should they have a family right away or should they put it off?

Without any experience in these matters, it's very difficult for them to make a decision.

Therefore, I've decided to start a little business on the side.

I'm calling it Rent-A-Kid and the idea is so simple I'm surprised somebody hasn't thought of it before.

I plan to rent out my kids to childless couples so they can see for themselves what being a parent is all about.

For five dollars a day, I'll provide Stephen, seven, who is my oldest.

I guarantee Stephen will bring home snakes, never comb his hair, grind plasticine into your best rug and never hear you when you talk to him.

Yes, all that for just five dollars.

Stephen has two jobs around the house: he gives the dog a drink every morning and he makes his bed.

Since he has conned the kid across the street, a boy named Brian, into watering the dog, we can forget about that.

Now, about the bed.

My wife looked at Stephen's bed the other day and commented on what a bad job he had done of making it.

"It's Richard's fault," he revealed, Richard being his two-year-old brother.

"What has Richard got to do with it?" my wife asked.

"Richard was in the bed when I made it," Stephen said. "And he kept wiggling."

Next I have my daughter, Jane, who is five and available for $3.98 per diem.

Jane is a perfect example of what a couple can expect in a daughter. She collects garbage and hides it in her "corner"; she loves perfume, eye makeup and lace panties; and she wants a brassiere as soon as she can grow some "elbows" which is how she describes a bosom.

Jane gave me this lesson about life the other day.

"If you find a better man, you don't keep the one you've got," she said. "You get a vorce."

"A vorce?" I asked.

"She means divorce," my wife chirped in.

And then my stock includes Richard who is two. I plan to charge at least twenty-five dollars a day for him.

Couples that see him often vow never to even hold hands again the rest of their lives. He is our version of The Pill.

Richard swings from drapes, writes on the dog and tries to put his sister in the diswasher.

He also falls off walls, jumps into swimming pools (he can't swim) and throws stones at the big hornet's nest in the tree in our front yard.

The other day I caught him stuffing a pencil down the bathroom sink.

"Don't do that!" I said.

"Have to," he answered.

"Why do you have to?" I asked.

"To get my penny," he explained.

You see, he had stuck this penny down the drain and was trying to . . . oh, never mind. I get this awful headache when I even think about it.

So there's my plan.

If you want to rent the entire set, I'll let them go for thirty dollars a day. You can have the three of them for ten dollars if you promise to keep them over a weekend.

And I'll give you fifty dollars if you want them Monday through Friday.

Just call Rent-A-Kid.

# A Mother Is . . .

A MOTHER KNOWS WHERE THE OTHER SOCK IS.

A mother blows on your cut after applying iodine.

A mother lets you win.

A mother wants to watch dancing or some other sissy stuff on TV instead of *The Hulk*.

A mother keeps your kindergarten stories in a special envelope in the cedar chest.

A mother can't throw overhand.

A mother can tell what you're doing downstairs even when you try to be quiet.

A mother eats cold toast for breakfast.

A mother has room in her bed at three o'clock in the morning if you've had a nightmare.

A mother puts her hand on your forehead if you say you're not hungry.

A mother can't whistle with her fingers.

A mother doesn't embarrass you in front of friends by kissing you.

A mother sews up the hole in the knee of your new pants before your father sees it.

A mother listens to your dinosaur project twenty-seven times, and always seems interested.

A mother never gets the last piece of pie.

A mother sews on Cub badges.

A mother always asks you why your sister is crying.

A mother wants to know what your best friend's mother gave you for lunch, and if you said, "Thank you."

A mother doesn't laugh when you cry.

A mother thinks you should wear an undershirt.

A mother, when you say you have nothing to do, always replies, "Why don't you clean up your room?"

A mother can't get the tops off bottles.

A mother feels soft.

A mother always wants to know where you're going.

A mother, when you spill something at the dinner table, always tells your father, "It was just an accident."

A mother doesn't like talking to your friends when she's having a bath.

A mother wishes you'd eat porridge.

A mother dances around the kitchen when she's happy.

A mother sticks your best schoolwork on the refrigerator door.

A mother says you can't have a kitten.

A mother asks now and then for a cuddle.

A mother has to explain to the lady down the street that you didn't start the fight first.

A mother gets a funny look in her eye when somebody says how fast you're growing up.

A mother is good at scratching backs . . .

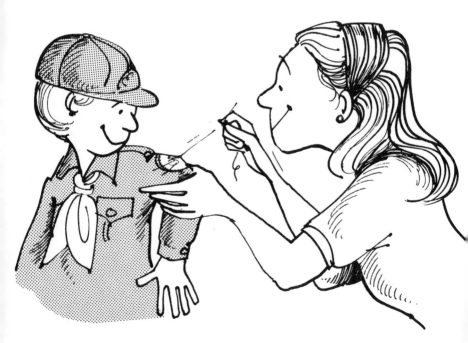

# Want To T-P-Y-R-A-B-S?

MY DAUGHTER JANE (WHO IS FIVE) WAS GIVING THE GRACE before dinner last night and this is what she said:

"God is great. God is good.

Thank you for the lovely men."

What do you think? Can she be helped? Do you think she's seeing too much of her mother?

Then there was the incident the other day when I caught her taking a poke at her little brother.

"Don't punch your brother!" I scolded.

"I didn't punch him," Jane replied.

"Don't lie. I saw you." I told her.

"I didn't punch him," Jane insisted. "I just gave him a pat in the mouth."

What are my chances of surviving a diabolical mind like that?

Jane came home from school and gave me this lesson on living.

"Donna calls everybody 'mental.' That means you don't go in other people's garages," Jane reported.

I haven't told you the whole story. There's another problem. His name is Richard and he just turned three.

We spell a lot when he's around because we don't want him to catch on to what we're saying. But he's turned the tables on us.

Last week Richard came up to me and said: "I want to go out and T-P-Y-R-A-B-S."

"What's 'T-P-Y-R-A-B-S'?" I wanted to know.

"You know—play," he informed me.

He was in an awful state recently and ran up to me in tears, holding up his thumb in obvious distress.

"Did you hurt your thumb?" I asked.

I JUST
GAVE HIM
A PAT IN
THE MOUTH...

"No," he said. "I want to suck my thumb and I can't find my blanket."

You see, he won't suck his thumb unless . . . do you think a quiet room at the YMCA for a week or so might help?

Richard was telling me the story of *The Three Little Pigs* before bed the other night.

When he came to the part where the pigs set off to build their homes, Richard revealed, "One went down the road to the right and one went down the road to the wrong."

There was a lot of noise downstairs last Saturday and I shouted, "Richard! What are you doing down there?"

There was a silence.

"What are you doing, Richard?" I repeated.

"I'm just looking to see," he finally reported.

And, you haven't suffered until you've had a three-year-old swing by a rope from the hall railing, yelling, "Tar-than!"

My other boy Stephen (who just turned eight) explained it

pretty well the other night after we had been out visiting a neighbor for about half-an-hour.

"Any calls?" I asked.

"No," he said. "But lots of close ones."

# Hi, California Ranch!

LIFE IN THE SUBURBS ISN'T EASY.

For example, I was at a meeting at the school the other evening when a woman gushed up to me and said, "You don't know me but I know you."

My face must have been blank because she didn't even pause.

"I'm the apple green split-level with a ravine lot at the end of the street," she revealed.

"Oh," I replied. "I'm . . ."

"Don't tell me!" she interrupted. "I know. You're the California ranch with the sun deck. I go past you every day on the way to the nursery school."

"I'm sorry," I said. "I didn't quite catch who you were."

"The apple green split-level." she repeated. "Maybe you know my husband. He's the dark green T-bird with whitewalls and air conditioning."

Finally, I caught on.

People in the suburbs aren't named after grandfathers, Old Testament prophets or even New York Yankee outfielders.

They're named after their possessions.

"So that's your husband," I replied, getting into the swing

of the conversation. "I've seen the T-Bird a hundred times but I always connected it to the Cape Cod on the corner with the swimming pool."

"No, the Cape Cod is married to the Mercedes," my neighbor corrected.

"Then where does the Starfire convertible live?"

"In the Spanish contemporary with the circular drive, the one with the treed lot and the color TV antenna," she explained. "Unfortunately, they don't get along."

"I'm sorry to hear that," I said.

"It's just a rumor," she confided, "but I hear he's fooling around with the two-storey colonial on the next street. I'd hate to be there the night the Buick station wagon comes home and catches the Starfire in the driveway."

"It could be nasty," I agreed.

"By the way, have I ever met your wife?" my neighbor asked.

"I don't know," I answered. "She's the white Austin Mini, the one with the dent in the rear fender."

"I can't place her off hand," she said.

"She's at the garage getting new points right now," I added.

"How about children?"

"Three," I said. "A bicycle, a tricycle and a doll buggy."

"I think I've seen the tricycle playing in your driveway when I've gone by," she said. "Why don't you send him down to my place some afternoon? I've got a wagon the same age."

"It sounds wonderful," I replied. "I'll send Richard. I mean, the tricycle."

# No Cavity Turtle

I'VE ALWAYS TOLD MY SON—THAT'S STEPHEN, WHO IS eight—anyway, I've always told him to make sure he brushes after meals.

This morning I walked into the bathroom and Stephen was brushing—but what he was brushing was his pet turtle.

They were taking turns on the toothbrush.

First Stephen's teeth, then the turtle's shell.

Stephen told me he didn't want his turtle to get cavities either.

Is that why I get these headaches? Yes, they're back again. They started to kick up last week—right after I had that heart-to-heart talk with Richard.

You know Richard. He's the baby—just turned 3.

Anyway, Richard has a slight lisp. For example, we ordered a new pair of Batman slippers for him and every time anybody came to the door, Richard would ask: "Are you the thlipper man?"

It went on for three days.

But that's not the problem. The problem is he's playing too much with his sister. And, because she's older—five—she always wants him to play girls' games.

I didn't worry, until I asked Richard the other day what he wanted to be when he grows up.

"I want to be a printheth," he thaid, I mean said.

He talks funny in other ways, too. I picked him up just yesterday and he commented: "Isn't I'm heavy?"

Is that any way for my son to talk?

We were out for a ride in the car last Sunday and he put his hands over the heater outlet to get them warm.

"Is there a dragon down there?" he wanted to know.

Maybe it's television. We took Stephen to the doctor last week—no, only three or four stitches in his chin. Well, he should know better than to slide on the hardwood floors in his stocking feet.

Anyway, Richard was in the waiting room when the nurse walked past.

"She's got dandruff," he announced in a loud voice, just the way they do in the commercials.

Jane turned to Richard and said, "Stop yelling. I'm not blind."

She worries me. She wants fancy underwear, high heels, lipstick—and that's to go to kindergarten.

All she talks about is getting married. Maybe that's natural. But do most five-year-old girls close their eyes when they kiss their teddy bears goodnight?

"I wish I knew how to make people," Jane grumbled the other day at the dinner table.

"Why?" I asked.

"Then I'd make another beautiful Jane," she replied.

# Aquarium in the Sky

THERE WAS A CRISIS AT THE HOUSE THIS WEEK BUT, fortunately, it worked out all right.

Several months ago my son, Stephen, bought a tiny turtle at the five-and-dime store and immediately named him Captain Cook.

Each day he washed Captain Cook's bowl. He put the captain in the sunshine. And he fed his quarter-sized friend with great devotion.

Needless to say, Captain Cook flourished and each day Stephen told us of the turtle's latest antics—how he had made a particularly amusing dive, how he had looked at him and blinked, how he had enjoyed a run on the bedroom floor.

Yesterday my wife was cleaning out Stephen's room and she noticed Captain Cook flopped over in his bowl and suspiciously still.

He was very, very dead.

Stephen, fortunately, was at school and had no inkling of his personal tragedy.

And a good thing.

He is given to taking wounded birds to the school nurse or bringing home lame frogs for first aid or begging tidbits for passing pussy cats.

My wife realized she would have one very sad son on her hands when he discovered the fate of his Captain Cook.

So she put the remains in her purse and drove to the nearest store with a stock of turtles.

And there she spent the next hour trying to find a turtle that matched Captain Cook.

Some were too big. Others lacked the spots of color near the ears. Others were the wrong shade of green.

Finally, she came up with one that wasn't exactly a twin but was the best stand-in of the bunch.

The bogus Captain Cook was then rushed home and deposited in the turtle bowl before Stephen came home from school.

Now came the moment of truth.

Stephen was in his room changing into his play clothes when he took the turtle out for his daily cleanout, stroll and feeding.

He gave "Captain Cook" a studied look and then called his mother.

"Captain Cook looks different," he said.

"What do you mean?" his mother asked innocently.

"His tail looks longer," Stephen commented.

"Maybe he's just stretching," was the careful answer.

My wife then came up with a story about applying a coat of special paint to the shell to give it extra strength.

"His shell underneath looks darker, too."

"Mom" he said, "are you sure this is Captain Cook?"

"Of course," she replied.

Frankly, I don't think he believed her but often in this world what we are looking for is a little lie, not the truth.

"Look, Mom," he said a moment later. "Look at Captain Cook dive! Isn't he neat?"

# Comic Book Solomon

CHILDREN ARE LITTLE HOARDERS AT HEART AND SELDOM interested in sharing. They see. They want. They keep.

My five-year-old daughter was listing off her possessions the other day when she brought out her supply of comic books.

"This is mine and this is mine and this is mine and . . ." she droned on picking up each comic book separately.

"Wait a minute," my wife said. "That one isn't yours. That's Richard's."

"No, it isn't. It's mine," Jane insisted.

"It's Richard's. It's got his name written on the top."

"It's mine."

"It isn't yours. Look. It has R-I-C-H-A-R-D written right there."

The evidence wasn't accepted.

"I don't care. It's my pile of comic books and it's mine," Jane persisted.

"You have to give it back to Richard," my wife countered.

"No."

"Wouldn't you be mad if Richard had something of yours and wouldn't give it to you?"

Jane then burst into tears, her answer for practically every argument.

"But it's mine!" she blubbered. "Grandma gave it to me."

"Grandma didn't give it to you. Richard got it at Christmas. I can remember . . . well, I can recognize Santa Claus's printing. He printed each of your names on a comic book for your stocking."

More tears. More yowls. More Bette Davis. And a tighter grasp on Exhibit A.

The prosecution proceeded to clinch its case by calling upon an independent witness (Jane's older brother, Stephen) and asking him to verify the name on the comic book.

"Richard," he swore.

Even Perry Mason couldn't have helped Jane after that damaging testimony.

The verdict.

"You've got to give the comic book back to Richard," my dishpan Hammurabi decreed.

Then followed a long discourse on the rights of others, the many advantages of being honest (especially in the afterlife) and, finally, the promise of a spanking if Jane didn't cough up the comic book.

"Now, for the last time, whose book is that?" my wife asked.

"Richard's," Jane admitted sullenly.

Richard was then summoned from the backyard.

"Go on," my wife encouraged Jane. "You know what you have to do."

"Here's your comic book, Richard," Jane said.

"I don't want it," Richard replied, running off to rejoin his pals.

Next case.

# Free Enterprise

IT'S PRETTY OBVIOUS MY KIDS INTEND TO GET GOVERNMENT jobs when they grow up. In fact, they've already started their training.

Yesterday they decided to set up a stand on the front lawn and sell sweets and strawberry drinks to passers-by.

It was a classic government operation.

The first thing the kids did was give themselves fancy titles.

Jane was named Candy Lady; Richard received the appointment of Chief Helper; Stephen was satisfied to take the position of Head Man.

Next they enlisted the services of two ordinary citizens (their mother and me).

All they wanted the volunteers to do was prepare the drinks, make a few dozen cookies, whip up some fudge, find the paper cups, cart some chairs and a table to the front lawn and take care of the expenses.

Head Man, Candy Lady and Chief Helper could handle the rest.

Proceeds, we were informed, would go to a good cause, probably the Junior Red Cross or "to some poor children."

Sales were very brisk, thanks to Chief Helper.

He came into the house several times to ask for money so he could buy fudge from Candy Lady.

And Candy Lady was delighted to learn Head Man would sell her drinks at wholesale prices—three cents a glass instead of the five cents charged the regular public.

Fortunately, Head Man didn't charge when he dipped into the stock himself so we saved that much.

The first non-Lautens customer was Ricky who lives across the street and has a very good appetite.

I was positive Head Man would make a killing.

Instead, Head Man offered Ricky full partnership in the stand and they had a drink and piece of fudge to seal the deal.

Brian suggested that a few games, operated as a sideline, might be a profitable addition to the enterprise so he got the job of Games Boy.

Naturally Brian wanted a break for Alan and Karen because they are his brother and sister and Head Man decided a free drink and two cookies would be fair.

About this time Candy Lady informed her mother that supplies were running short and could she do something about it.

And a few more chairs would be nice, too.

Pretty soon my wife was back at work over the stove, I was lugging furniture around and we had a lawn full of kids having a whale of a time, eating, drinking and playing.

By the end of the afternoon, my wife and I were bushed, we were out of pocket $3.50 and the lawn was a mess.

Total proceeds (according to Head Man) were thirty-seven cents.

And if that doesn't sound like a government operation, I don't know what does.

# Sex and Dragonflies

I CAN RECALL MY FIRST MAN-TO-MAN TALK ABOUT SEX AS IF it were yesterday.

Actually, it's almost a week now. But I'm still shaky.

"You'd better talk to Stephen about the facts of life," my wife said. "He's been asking questions."

"But why me?" I protested.

"Because you're his father," she explained.

"But . . ."

"I don't want to hear another word," my wife interrupted. "I'll get Stephen."

Stephen came into the room.

My hands began to perspire, I could feel a twitch developing in my left eye and I had to clear my throat several times.

"Mom says you want to see me," Stephen opened.

"Yes," I replied. "Sit down."

"Could you hurry, Dad? Brian's waiting for me."

"This won't take long," I began. "I just thought you and I should have a little talk. I thought maybe you'd like to ask me some, well, questions about things."

"No, I don't," Stephen replied. "Can I go now? Brian and me are . . ."

"Brian and I," I corrected.

"Brian and I are going down to the creek to catch bugs," Stephen told me.

"Bugs! That brings up a very important question, Stephen. Do you know where bugs come from?" I asked.

"From the grass around the creek," he answered.

"I mean, do you know how they're born?"

"Not exactly," he confessed. "Do you?"

"No," I said. "I hoped you might."

"Can you hurry, Dad? Brian's going to go home if I don't come out soon."

Throwing discretion to the wind, I went directly to the point. "Do the boys and girls at school ever discuss, well, boys and girls. You know—sex," I finally blurted.

"Sometimes," Stephen confessed. "I caught a dragonfly yesterday, Dad. Brian and me . . . I mean, Brian and I are keeping him in a jar."

"I don't want you to think that it's dirty or shameful," I said. "It's beautiful. And you should never be ashamed or embarrassed about something that's beautiful."

"What's beautiful, Dad?" Stephen asked.

"It's beautiful," I explained. "What we're talking about."

"You mean dragonflies or sex?" he wanted to know.

"The second one," I answered.

"Oh. Can I go down to the creek now or do you want to talk some more about sex?" Stephen requested.

"Your mother thinks we should talk," I said.

And, for the next ten minutes, that's what we did.

I looked Stephen straight in the shoulder and told him all I knew about life and kissing and girls and babies. I didn't hold anything back.

When I finally looked up, there was a pained expression on Stephen's face.

"What's the matter?" I asked, fearing I had said too much.

"My foot's asleep," Stephen replied. "Besides, Brian's gone home."

# Cleanliness is Next to Impossible

I HAVE ONE CHILD WHO'S A DREAM. JANE PICKS UP. SHE
makes her bed. She's polite. She eats everything on her plate.
And she never jumps on my stomach when I'm asleep on the
chesterfield.

Jane's only fault is that she's not an only child.

You see, she has two brothers—Richard and Stephen—and
they are rotten to the core. They are so rotten that when they
pick up a toad, the toad gets warts.

Richard and Stephen fight. They tease. They won't change
their socks. They wipe their noses on anything that's
handy—tablecloths, shirt-tails, the family dog.

Grubby? My kids are so grubby that the White Knight
detours when he comes to our block. Mr. Clean actually had
a full head of hair until he tried to get my kids to wash.

When my wife housecleans in their room, she doesn't use a
broom; she uses a rake. We've got the only room in the
country with wall-to-wall underwear.

Anyway, I came up with a terrific plan to get the two boys
in line.

"Starting today, we're going to have a new system around
here," I announced at the breakfast table.

Richard (who is three) looked at me and crossed his eyes.
Stephen (who is eight) kept reading his comic book. And
Jane (who is six) looked up, folded her hands in her lap and
paid perfect attention.

"I'm going to award cash prizes to the best children in this
family every week," I continued.

At the word "cash" everybody settled down and Richard
uncrossed his eyes.

"I'm going to award twenty-five cents to the child who
keeps the neatest room and helps most around the house."

"I'm going to award ten cents to the child who eats his meals and shows the best manners at the dinner table."

"And I'm going to give an additional ten cents to the child who cleans his, or her, teeth most regularly," I concluded.

"How much does that come to?" Stephen (who is saving up for some kind of plastic thing-maker) wanted to know.

"If you're best in all three categories, you can get forty-five cents," I explained.

"Goody," he said, rushing off to brush his teeth, giving his brother a perfect elbow in the ear so he could get into the bathroom first.

"Maybe I should have made an award for the boy who throws the fewest elbow smashes, too," I said to my wife.

"Don't overdo it," she whispered. "But I like the idea. I like the idea of appealing to their competitive spirit, or giving them a challenge, of working on their psyches."

"I'm working on their greed and you know it," I corrected. "This is out-and-out bribery but what the hell, nothing else has worked."

My wife put a chart in the kitchen and revealed she would give stars every day (a gold star for three points, a silver for two, etc.) and that Friday would be awards day.

Well, I'd like to report that my plan worked perfectly, but it wasn't quite that way.

Stephen made a great start. He cleaned up his room, made his bed and even picked up the eighty-six sets of underwear scattered on the floor.

But then he didn't want to use his bed the rest of the week.

"It'll get messed again if I sleep in it," he complained. "Why can't I just sleep on the chesterfield in the front room?"

We told him he was missing the entire spirit of the contest and ordered him to sleep in his own bed.

By the middle of the week, Stephen's room was back to

normal—rumpled bed, his entire wardrobe laid out on the floor, bits and pieces of a chemistry set everywhere.

"Your room's a mess," I mentioned. "You won't win that way."

"Jane's so far ahead I can't catch up," Stephen replied. "So I might as well save myself for next week. I think I'll go out and play."

Richard? He never even got that far. He threw in the towel, or the underwear, if you prefer, the very first day.

So there you have it.

Stephen and Richard still live in disaster areas. They brush when they remember. The eat if they feel like it.

Meanwhile, Jane's room is still neat as a pin. She still eats everything on her plate. She still brushes after meals—and sits with her hands folded in her lap when I talk to her.

Only now it costs me forty-five cents every week.

# Leaving Home—Sort Of

WE HAD ANOTHER CRISIS THIS WEEK.

Jane left home.

She put on her best dress; she packed her bags and she struck out on her own.

A six-year-old girl doesn't have to put up with spankings and baby brothers and a lot of other indignities.

So there!

But let me go back to the beginning.

My wife caught Jane throwing some nifty punches at her brother Richard (who has just turned four) down in the playroom.

Jane claimed Richard had slugged her first. Richard said she was nuts. Anyway, Jane had been making faces at him. Jane said she wouldn't make faces if Richard would stop calling her teacher "Miss Schnook." Her name, Jane pointed out, is "Miss Shook."

My wife settled the case out of court.

Smack! Smack!

And right on the bare legs, too.

Richard took the punishment like a true man. He rushed to his room and stuffed his blue blanket up his nose.

Jane, however, was incensed.

"I'm leaving home," she announced with her hands on her hips.

"Go ahead," my wife bargained.

"And I'm never coming back," Jane vowed.

"Don't forget to write," my wife replied.

"I won't write," Jane guaranteed.

"Suit yourself," my wife shrugged.

Jane then stomped into her room, muttering to herself. She began tossing a few belongings into an overnight bag. Just necessities—underwear, her best doll, a partly-licked grape sucker, a nightie (the one with the lace on it) and her piggy bank.

"Well, I'm going," she repeated when she reached the door, giving us one last chance to reconsider her reckless decision.

"Goodbye," my wife said, hardly looking up.

That was the point of no return. The two of them were committed and nobody was going to give in.

Jane walked to the front door and she was gone.

My wife jumped up and ran into the front room, where she hid behind the curtains.

"Jane's walking down the walk," she whispered. "She's looking back at the house. Keep down! She's crossing to the other side of the street."

My wife lost sight of Jane for a few moments and raced into the bathroom to get a different vantage point.

"Jane's going over to Karen's," my wife continued. "Karen must be out. Her mother's talking to Jane. Oh! Jane is crossing the road again. She's going around the corner . . ."

This play-by-play report went on for about twenty-five minutes.

My wife rushed from one side of the house to another, always keeping one eyeball ahead of Jane.

And then Jane started to walk toward our house again.

"Quick! Pretend you're reading the paper, or something," my wife ordered as she sprinted past me.

That wasn't difficult since I was already reading the paper at the time.

"And don't say a thing," she added.

My wife then rushed into the kitchen, where she turned on some taps, rattled dishes and made herself look very busy.

Jane walked into the house.

Jane walked down to her room.

And Jane didn't say a word. But I could hear her unpacking.

A few minutes later Jane walked into the kitchen.

"I'm back," she revealed.

"That's nice," my wife said.

Pause.

"Do you know why I came back?" Jane finally asked.

"No," my wife admitted.

"Because I love you," Jane said.

"Dinner will be ready in about ten minutes," my wife said, turning away and blowing her nose a couple of times. Hard.

"What's wrong, Mom?" Jane asked.

"I've got something in my eye," my wife explained.

I guess I'll never understand women—not even the six-year-olds.

# That Richard

OUR FOUR-YEAR-OLD'S NAME IS RICHARD. BUT WE NEVER call Richard, Richard.

As far as we're concerned his first name is That.

He is That Richard Lautens.

When I come home from work, for example, the first thing my wife always says to me is, "Do you know what That Richard did today?"

Neighbors comment, "That Richard is sure a live wire, isn't he?"

And a thousand times every weekend when I hear a silence in the house, I shout, "Where's That Richard?"

I know he's up to something.

In any case, "That Richard" is his name, regardless of what it says on his birth certificate. And no hyphen, please.

Which may explain what I've got to say.

The news has just been brought to me: That Richard's in trouble again.

"Do you know what That Richard just did?" his brother Stephen asked. "He took my toothbrush, rubbed it in soap and then dunked it in the toilet—twice."

As an afterthought, Stephen suggested: "When I catch That Richard, I'm going to kill him."

But That Richard is nowhere to be found. Undoubtedly he's hiding in some closet or barricaded behind the chester-field sucking on his blue blanket.

Whenever there's any kind of crisis in his life, which is always, That Richard always resorts to his blue blanket.

He puts his thumb in his mouth, stuffs the corner of his blanket up his nose—and then he's ready to face all comers.

Frankly, we're ashamed of the blanket.

It's been washed, patched and mended. It's been used as a

whip, rope, tent, trampoline, Batman's cape and God-only-knows what else.

It's been dragged hundreds of miles. It's been snapped, skipped and soaked.

And it looks it.

The man at the service station uses a better cloth to clean my windshield. If the Board of Health ever spots it, we're all going to be condemned.

We've tried to break That Richard of the habit but our efforts to date have failed.

Take the last time.

Somebody suggested we should cut off a corner of the blanket and give that to you-know-who as a mini-substitute. Then, while he's not looking, gradually cut more and more off until he's left with just a couple of threads.

Presto! No more blanket. Just one normal, well-adjusted, disarmed kid.

Well, it sounded like a sure thing until That Richard was over at the supermarket with his mother and began bawling his head off.

The manager of the store rushed over to see what the trouble was. That Richard explained he has lost his "ko-knee"—which is his baby-talk way of saying "corner", meaning the corner of the blanket.

"Where is your ko-knee, little man?" the manager asked.

That Richard just pointed to the meat counter—about forty feet of gleaming meat counter

He had stuffed his patch of blanket down one of the little cracks—he wasn't sure which one—and he wasn't going to budge until he got it back.

About forty minutes later the counter was in pieces and so was the manager. Finally he discovered a scrap of cloth big enough to cover a gnat, provided the gnat didn't sleep in a double bed.

"Is this it?" the manager wanted to know.

Without a word, That Richard took the cloth, stuffed it up his nose, and walked away.

Since then we've made sure he carries the entire blanket. At least it won't fit down cracks in the meat counter.

I don't know why the toughest of all our kids should need a blanket. That Richard will take on the entire block in tackle football. He loves to swing on his curtains and make Tarzan yells. He wrestles our 200-pound dog. And wins.

It's very deceiving.

Just the other day my wife was over at the plaza getting a pair of shoes for That Richard, who moves so fast he wears them out from the inside, too.

My wife watched as the clerk tried a pair on That Richard's feet.

"Will these shoes wear well?" she asked.

The shoe salesman looked at That Richard, who was sucking on his blanket and looking like a perfect angel, or sissy.

"Madam," he said. "These shoes are Savage."

"So is he," my wife replied.

# Stephen Spendo

ONE OF THE GREAT LESSONS EVERY PARENT TRIES TO TEACH
his children is the value of money.

You know the pitch.

Daddy works hard for his money. Money doesn't grow on
trees. A penny saved is a penny earned. Put your money
away for a rainy day.

And a lot of other catchy phrases like that.

Well, with that in mind, we have had the children on the
weekly payroll for some time now. Yes, allowances.

Stephen (who is eight) gets twenty-five cents a week; Jane
(who is six) gets ten cents; and Richard (who is four) gets five
cents.

In addition, as I mentioned before, the kids can earn
bonuses for cleaning their teeth, eating their meals, keeping
a neat room and not biting each other any place it shows.

The prize money totals forty-five cents—but I throw in an
extra five cents if anybody can perform a grand slam and top
all divisions of the competition.

Every Saturday morning the kids line up for their loot.

We have no trouble with Jane. She takes her dough and
runs into her bedroom, where she counts it and then hides it
under a loose floorboard or something.

She, in a word, is a saver.

Richard is different. First of all, he seldom gets any bonus.
Unless we give money for fist fighting, there is no way Richard is ever going to get rich.

So he takes his five cents and usually loses it, swallows it or
tries to stuff it up his nose.

But Stephen is something else.

Stephen likes to spend. He is drawn to stores like a mag-
net. He is so good at getting rid of money I'm sure he's going
to wind up in government, probably with CBC.

Anyway, we've been working on Stephen, trying to get him to keep his money in a large piggy bank instead of at the plaza.

If I say so myself, we weren't doing too badly.

Stephen must have had five or six dollars in his bank. But, apparently, the strain was too much on him.

"I'd like to take some money out of my bank," Stephen informed his mother when he reached that financial pinnacle.

"Why?" she asked.

"Because there's something I want to buy," he admitted.

"Ste-phen!" my wife began.

She always breaks his name in the middle that way when she's annoyed—and he knows it.

"Ste-phen!" she said. "Why can't you leave your money alone? You're just starting to save nicely and now you want to go out and spend it on something foolish."

"It's not foolish, Mom," he promised.

"Stephen, you always say that," my wife complained. "You can find more ways to spend money than any boy I know. Why does money burn a hole in your pocket? Why can't you save like your sister?"

"I don't know, Mom," he replied. "Can I have my money now?"

"You realize, Stephen, if you spend your money you won't be able to get that microscope you said you wanted to save for?"

"Yes," Stephen said.

"If you saved just a few more weeks you could get a light for your bicycle," she continued.

"I know," Stephen answered. "But there's something I want to get now."

"I give up," my wife surrendered. "Get your bank. Take the money out. But don't come to me when you're broke. You've got to learn the value of money."

Stephen took the rubber plug out of the piggy bank's

stomach, emptied it to the last penny, and walked out of the house.

"I don't know what we're going to do about Stephen," my wife muttered. "He just won't save."

"Mmmm," I commented, a comment I find very useful when I don't want to take sides.

"He only thinks of today. For Stephen, there's no tomorrow," she nattered.

"Mmm," I said.

And then my wife went back to the kitchen, still muttering about Stephen the Spendthrift, her wastrel son, the Diamond Jim of the sucker set.

About an hour later Stephen walked into the house with a package in his hand.

"This is for you," he said, handing it to his mother.

"What is it?" she asked.

"Open it," he begged.

Well, she did. And inside a blue box, folded in white tissue paper, was a pair of earrings.

"I saw them in a store yesterday and thought you'd like them," Stephen explained.

Stephen's mother didn't reply. She just gave Stephen a big hug.

The earrings turn my wife's earlobes a little green, but on special occasions, those are the earrings she always wears.

After all, they represent the lifetime savings of a young boy—and his love.

What can be more precious than that?

# What Are You Doing? . . . *Nothing!*

WILL ALL THE NEW PARENTS IN THE AUDIENCE PLEASE RAISE their hands?

Ah, yes.

Well, this is for you.

Right now you're only worrying about the little tyke throwing up on your new suit or getting that funny look on his face when you've got company and you're passing him (or her) around.

But pretty soon baby will learn to talk and that's when the real fun begins.

You're going to discover that children can talk all right—but what they say has no connection with what they mean.

Let me explain.

Very soon you'll hear a crashing silence downstairs in the rec room (parents quickly recognize silence as a danger signal) and you'll ask:

"What are you doing, Harry?"

I will bet you one million dollars that little Harry will reply, "Nothing!"

That is the standard answer all kids give.

But what exactly does "nothing" mean?

"Nothing" means little Harry is scribbling on the walls with a marker pen, sawing through the legs of your pool table or trying to plug the family cat's tail into a wall socket.

With that explanation, I'm now going to attempt to give you new parents an interpretation of some of the other things you'll hear in the next few years.

*Question:* Why is Susie crying?

*Answer:* I don't know.

*Translation:* Susie is crying because I judo-chopped her in the mouth, ate her candy bar and told her there's a big ghost hiding behind the curtains waiting to swallow her up.

*Question:* Do you have to go to the bathroom before I do up your snowsuit?

*Answer:* No.

*Translation:* Yes.

*Question:* Who left these wet boots on the hardwood floor I just waxed?

*Answer:* Susie did.

*Translation:* Susie did. I left my wet boots on the new broadloom in the front room. The only thing I left on the hardwood floor was a coat, hat and the one mitt I've got left.

*Question:* Can anyone go to the store for me?

*Answer:* I'm busy.

*Translation:* I'm watching Willie Weirdo and the Unimaginables on TV and I've only seen this particular show thirty-four times.

*Question:* Are you sure the shoes fit?

*Answer:* They fit.

*Translation:* They don't fit but I'm not going to complain until tomorrow when they're scuffed up and the store won't take them back.

*Question:* Did you remember to flush?

*Answer:* Yes.

*Translation:* In fact, I flushed seven times. It took that many to flush down my toothbrush, a powder puff, two rolls of tissue and a china figurine that's been in the family seventy-five years.

*Question:* Has anybody seen the china figurine I had on my dresser?

*Answer:* No.

*Translation:* (See above.)

*Question:* Were you a good boy at Grandma's?

*Answer:* Grandma says I was a very good boy.

*Translation:* I raised hell all day but Grandma did say I was a good boy. (Grandmothers always say their grandchildren

are good and are completely unreliable as character references.)

_Question:_ What are you doing in the bathroom?
_Answer:_ I'm washing.
_Translation:_ I'm washing—I'm washing the walls, the floor,
the medicine cabinet, the door. And I'm using the good
towels as a washcloth and the scented soap that's seventy-five
cents a cake.

_Question:_ Are you getting into trouble?
_Answer:_ No.
_Translation:_ No. I already am in trouble.

*Question:* Who broke the lamp?

*Answer:* I was just playing quietly when Susie and her friends came in and they started to wrestle and fight and call me names and I told them to stop and they wouldn't and they made a face at me and I told them I was going to call my mother but you weren't around so I couldn't call you and I didn't know what to do so I just tried to ignore them but they . . .

*Translation:* I did.

Anyway, those are a few tips that may come in handy. And, in the difficult days ahead, always remember one thing: your kids probably like you almost as much as they do the dog next door.

# Painting the Town Peanut Butter

IF YOU EVER WALKED INTO OUR HOME, YOU'D PROBABLY swear you were at RCMP headquarters.

In fact, we've got more fingerprints on file than the Mounties, the FBI and Scotland Yard combined—and all on the walls.

Our kids can't walk, talk, eat, watch TV or anything without leaving a telltale trail. Every day is Palm Sunday at our place.

Sometimes when I get home and look at the smudges I don't know which to get plastered first, me or the living-room wall.

Take Stephen.

His favourite lunch is a grape jelly sandwich. As a result, we have a lovely purple wall in the kitchen behind his place at the table.

Now I have nothing against purple.

But it clashes with the peanut butter splattered on Richard's side of the room.

And trust Jane to love pizza.

Have you ever tried to get curtains that match grape jelly, peanut butter and pizza?

Believe me, it's impossible.

Apparently there's another unwritten law in the Lautens residence: you can't sit on a chair. You have to lie on the floor and put your feet on the walls.

The only time my kids are erect is when they're eating grape jelly sandwiches, peanut butter, etc.

As a result, I have more tracks than CN.

The walls in the dining-room are supposed to be oyster but you couldn't bring that oyster back to life with mouth-to-mouth resuscitation.

Don't think I haven't tried to fight back. I've told the children that the floor is just a horizontal wall in the hope they might try to walk on that for a change.

I've also suggested they wash their hands at least once a week, whether they need it or not, figuring if I'm going to get the digit I might just as well go for a clean one.

It hasn't worked.

Finally, it got so bad I had to call in the painters this past week.

My suggestion was that we paint the entire house in some shade the children couldn't mark.

However, the paint charts don't have a color that exactly matches the stain left when a sock, worn for a week or so under a rubber boot, hits the wall and sort of slithers to the floor. We settled for cream.

The painter, a nice fellow named Ernie, finished the living-room the first day.

However, by the time he arrived the next morning, there were fingerprints all over the doorway leading to the kitchen.

By checking twirls, swirls and lifelines, we were able to determine it was Richard.

Besides, Richard had one cream hand and an ear to match.

"Kids will be kids," Ernie said, a little weakly, I thought. And he spent most of the morning scrubbing Richard's hand and his ear and repainting the door frame.

That afternoon it was Jane's turn.

She had to get something out of a downstairs closet. Not later. Now!

Anyway, she was searching in the closet when she brushed against the closet door and turned a blue velvet dress into a cream velvet dress.

Ernie got out the turpentine again. He got Jane cleaned up—and then gave the closet door another coat.

"You'll need three gallons for the house and four gallons for the kids at this rate," I joked.

"Ha, ha," Ernie replied without exactly rolling on the floor in amusement.

That night I really chased the kids. Every time they even looked at a wall or a door I yelled at them. I told them Ernie was sore, that I was sore and that they would be sore, too— on the behind—if they left any more marks.

Ernie was able to finish the painting in a couple of days and we were all just delighted that there was no trouble.

"I guess I was the only one who didn't get in the paint," Stephen gloated as Ernie was packing up to leave.

Unfortunately, Stephen was leaning on a wet wall when he said it.

Ernie unpacked.

# Three to Get Ready

# Kindergarten Crisis

THIS HAS BEEN CRAM WEEK AT OUR PLACE.

The Board of Education sent us a letter stating that Richard Gary Lautens, aged four, should know his name and address and telephone number before enrolling in kindergarten.

That's no sweat.

But he's also expected to tie his own shoelaces.

Well, I've got some bad news for the Board of Education.

Richard Gary Lautens can swim, climb fences, open the refrigerator door, print his name, change the channel on the TV set and do up his pants—but he can't tie his shoelaces.

We have worked with him for nearly ten days. We've shown him how to make loops. We have shown him where the knot goes.

But Richard Gary Lautens still can't figure it out.

If the kindergarten teacher gives the class a test today in shoelace tying, Richard Gary Lautens is going to flunk.

He may be a drop-out even before he's a drop-in.

During the summer he never wore shoes. Before that, he had loafer-style footwear that posed no problem.

So, if the Board of Education is listening, I want them to know he only needs a little experience.

I want them to give Richard Gary Lautens a second chance and not turf him out on the street or recommend that he be transferred to a trade school.

I'm sure he'll get the hang of it if they'll just be patient.

The reason I'm begging is simple: If they reject Richard Gary because he can't tie shoelaces, they'll break somebody's heart—my wife's.

For ten years she's dreamed of this glorious day.

When times were tough and she was up to her ascot in dirty diapers, she'd turn to me and sigh, "Some day these kids will be at school and I'll have some time to myself."

It was all that kept her going.

Well, today's the day.

Stephen is in grade five. Jane is in grade two. I've got a job. And Richard is in kindergarten, if the Board of Education isn't too picky.

That may not seem much to you but, to my wife, that adds up to 150 minutes of free time every day.

From 9 to 11:30, five mornings a week, my wife will have nobody underfoot, or under anything else, either.

That's 750 minutes every week not to make sandwiches, 750 minutes not to tell somebody to keep his hands off the walls, 750 minutes not to ask if they flushed.

My wife has oodles of plans for those 750 minutes so if the Board of Education doublecrosses her now, I'm not responsible for what she might do.

Personally, I'm sorry to see Richard Gary Lautens leave his babyhood behind.

My wife's more practical, however.

"If his kindergarten teacher didn't start on tranquilizers at least two weeks ago, she'll never catch up," she commented.

# Bedroom Rules

JANE IS THE ONLY ONE AT OUR HOUSE WHO REALLY KNOWS how to handle my wife.

That's because Jane has heart. She also has chin, which she sticks out whenever she gets involved in an argument.

For example, when my wife and I have a fight, I calmly explain my position with cold logic. Next I point out the weakness in what my wife has to say.

And then I apologize.

The boys are the same.

They are feathers off the old chicken.

But not Jane.

She could give a bulldog stubborn lessons. I would match her against Gibraltar any day.

In fact, when Jane and her mother lock eyeballs, the male members of the family hide behind the chesterfield to escape the fallout.

Let me explain just how Jane operates.

A few days ago my wife thought everyone was out of the house when she heard some noises coming from Jane's bedroom.

When she opened the door, she found Jane playing cut-outs with a little boy name Hugh.

Hugh is the one who hangs around the house and turns the skipping rope for Jane and puts her bike away in the garage if she's busy.

Like Jane, Hugh is only seven—but, as you can tell, he's perfect husband material.

Anyway, Jane was ordering Hugh around as usual, telling him what he could cut, which scissors he could use, and where to put all the scraps of paper that were on the floor.

In short, Jane was having a lovely time.

"What are you two doing?" my wife asked.

"Playing," Jane replied.

"That's nice," my wife said.

And then, figuring it's never too early to start breaking in the house rules, my wife added:

"If you're going to play with Hugh in your bedroom, make sure you leave the door open."

Jane was furious.

She couldn't care less about the bedroom door being open or closed.

But the idea of somebody coming into HER bedroom and giving HER orders!

And in front of Hugh!

Well, it was just too much for Jane to take.

Her chin almost bounced off the wall, it stuck out so far.

In any case, my wife thought that was the end of it and went back to the kitchen to her usual chores.

That night Jane was busier than ever in her room and the next morning we found out why.

On her bedroom door was posted this notice:

*Please do not disturb.*
*Knock first.*
*If nobody answers, no*
*one is here.*
*And please do not disturb.*

Not only was the message stuck to the door, it was written in black marker pencil on red paper so nobody could miss it.

My wife insisted I talk to Jane.

I took Jane aside and explained that it's polite to leave the bedroom door open when a young lady entertains a young man, especially when they're both seven.

I also assured her that we had only her best interests at heart.

Then I said her ponytail was coming along beautifully—that's always the clincher with Jane.

Anyway, she smiled.

Later that day she slipped a tiny piece of paper in my hand.

It read:

*Ticit to Jane's room.*

# You Dirty Rat!

MY DAUGHTER FINALLY ASKED THE QUESTION THAT STRIKES terror in every father's heart.

Oh, we know it's coming.

We can brace ourselves. We can rehearse our answers. We can tell ouselves it isn't the end of the world.

But all that goes out the window when your daughter looks you in the eye and says:

"Can I have a white rat, Daddy?"

It is a matter of record that every child in the entire world wants to own a white rat of his own, a rat he (or she) can hold and play with and feed and stick in the face of grownups.

It is just as provable that everybody over the age of twenty-one thinks that white rats are creepy.

But when you're a father, you're supposed to be fearless and brave and strong.

You're definitely not supposed to be afraid of an itty-bitty white rat with beady eyes and a long pink tail that wraps around your arm and is probably a distant relative of something that carried bubonic plague around Europe a couple of centuries ago.

The question is: how do you get out of keeping the rat and still keep your Galahad reputation intact?

Do you pick up the sinister creature when your daughter brings him home and lets him run up your arm and nibble on your nose?

Do you say he's terribly cute (through gritted teeth) and that it would be worth getting the Black Death just to have such a gorgeous pet?

And then do you explain that it would be heartless to take the wee fellow away from his brothers and sisters at the garbage dump?

Why, he'd pine away!

I did none of these things.

A neighbor and former friend named Garside gave our seven-year-old daughter a white rat and when Jane brought it home she was terribly excited.

"Look what I got!" she said. "It's a white rat and Mrs. Garside said I could have the cage, too, and he's real friendly and he doesn't take up much space and I promise to take care of him myself and he hardly eats at all and can I keep him?"

Alas! I lost my head and resorted to those three words that always get me out of a jam around the house:

"Ask your mother," I said.

Jane took the rat into the kitchen and her mother took care of the situation in twenty seconds flat.

"What's that ugly thing?" she asked.

"A rat," Jane began.

"Take him out of here," came the order.

"But . . ."

"Now!" Jane's mother insisted.

That was the end of the discussion.

"It's easy to be a mother" Jane muttered as she left the house to return the white rat. "All you have to be is crabby."

## The Fly in the Ice Cube

IF THERE'S ONE THING A NINE-YEAR-OLD BOY CAN'T RESIST it's a mail-order catalogue, especially one that promises "2,000 novelties PLUS useful and fun articles."

Stephen got his hands on such a booklet and I know exactly what he went through.

When I was a kid, my eyes popped, too, at the pages of neat items just waiting to be mailed out to me upon receipt of a money order and a small sum to cover the cost of handling, no postage stamps, please.

Alas, as every adult knows, a mail-order catalogue from a novelty firm is like a girl with false eyelashes, false hair and a padded bra—it advertises more than it can deliver.

However, nine-year-olds don't understand that fact of life.

Therefore, I couldn't blame Stephen for getting excited about the veritable cornucopia of delights at his fingertips.

"It's fun to get things by mail," the catalogue encouraged on its cover.

Why, you could get an engagement and wedding ring set—"for fun or for real" for a measly one dollar, with "an attractive plastic gift box" as a bonus.

Or, at $4.50, a young boy might purchase a telephone "snooper" and listen in to conversations like a secret agent.

Stephen didn't know what to mark down on his order form first.

Would it be the $2.50 microphone that would permit him to talk over the family radio and "imitate Bob Hope or Bing Crosby" at parties?

Would it be the $13.95 "lie detector machine . . . which registers emotions, feelings and reactions even when people try to conceal them?"

Or, for fifty cents, would he get the booklet on ju-jitsu and learn to "beat the bullies" with a devastating series of "kidney squeezes" and "throat grips," not to mention the "etc. etc." which is included with every lesson?

Obviously, Stephen could have made a decision in seconds if he possessed one of the company's $5.75 "mechanical brain computers" which are even capable of "playing games."

But all Stephen had to work with was the space between his own ears, and a very limited budget.

He finally decided on four items:

A plastic ice cube "with real bug—a real shocker when discovered in a drink!" Price—twenty-five cents.

Garlic (Awful!) Gum that "ruins the breath for hours." Package of five sticks—twenty cents.

Magnetic lodestone, regarded by many as "a lucky symbol" and often sold "for fabulous amounts!" Yours for fifty cents.

And finally, a "miracle light bulb that lights without wires—amazing, mystifying! A bargain at twenty-five cents.

Stephen figured all that stuff was probably better than the fake bullet holes or even the bleeding dagger, both of which he considered as possible purchases.

Anyway, he got his money and his order form and his letter—and sent away for the fabulous treasures.

The next few days were hell.

Stephen was certain that delivery—"speedy service!" the company promised—would be practically instantaneous.

A mailman couldn't turn our corner without Stephen's being on him and wanting to check through his pouch.

Finally, the big day arrived.

Stephen opened his package and the first thing he noticed was that his magic light bulb was a little small.

In the catalogue it looked large enough to light downtown Montreal but the cold truth of the matter was that it was only the size of a pea.

The lodestone looked like a very ordinary piece of gravel and, when Stephen rubbed it, no genie appeared out of the thin air. So much for "lucky" symbols.

He put a stick of the garlic gum in his mouth and breathed all over his brother—but his brother said it smelled nice and asked for some too.

However, I was the one who delivered the *coup de grace*.

That evening at the dinner table I was sipping a cool glass of iced tea. The kids were giggling but I didn't pay any attention.

Anyway, I finished the drink, put the glass down—and looked into a collection of the most disappointed eyes I've ever seen.

Yes, the plastic ice cube "with real bug" was in my glass and I hadn't noticed.

"Things aren't always what people say, are they, Dad?" Stephen commented at bedtime, more as a statement than a question.

I just smiled. Somehow, I think he got his money's worth out of that catalogue don't you?

# The Tooth Fairy Arrives — Late

I DON'T KNOW WHETHER YOU REALIZE IT OR NOT but the tooth fairy has upped her prices.

A few years ago the most you could get for a tooth under your pillow was a nickel—a dime at the outside.

But the going rate these days is a quarter.

I know because I've just had to put my money where Jane's mouth is.

Yes, even without teeth my kids can put the bite on me.

For weeks Jane went around with this loose tooth in the front of her mouth. She wiggled it. She moved it from side to side.

And, whenever we had something for dinner she didn't like, she'd point to it and say she couldn't possibly eat because her mouth was coming apart.

Obviously, she still had plenty of lip.

Jane really played the tooth for all it was worth and her brothers were green with envy, especially Stephen.

"When the tooth comes out, you'll be able to put it under your pillow and get money," he advised his sister, who didn't know about such things until he opened his big mouth.

Stephen is so money-hungry that he'd get his gums removed if he thought there was a buck in it.

Anyway, from then on, Jane knew she was walking around with a potential fortune right under her nose so she gave that tooth some pretty good tugs.

But it didn't budge.

Stephen, who is very brave when it comes to his sister's pain, said Jane should tie a string around the tooth, tie the string to a doorknob and . . .

I vetoed that.

"With my luck, the doorknob would come off," I told him.

So the tooth just dangled, and so did we.

A few days later we were at the breakfast table when Jane ran into the kitchen, sobbing her heart out.

"My tooth's gone," she blubbered, "but the tooth fairy didn't leave me any money."

My wife (who makes a career of telling it like it isn't) was horrified.

"When did the tooth come out?" she asked.

"Last night in bed," Jane sobbed.

"Why didn't you tell me?" my wife demanded.

"Because I wanted to surprise you," Jane explained. "I put my tooth under my pillow but I didn't get anything from the tooth fairy and my tooth's gone!"

Jane was crying her eyes out by now.

That's when my wife pulled the old let-me-take-a-look-to-make-sure-you're-right trick.

The two of them disappeared into Jane's bedroom.

A few minutes later Jane shouted, "I've found a quarter!"

She was ecstatic.

When we got a minute alone, I asked my wife how she had pulled it off.

"Easy," she said, "I palmed a quarter and slipped it into the pillowcase when Jane wasn't looking. Then . . ."

". . . then you suggested she shake the pillowcase," I broke in.

"Right," she admitted. "By the way, I found the tooth in

the covers and put it in your dresser drawer. Oh, yes. You owe me a quarter."

Frankly, I was a little annoyed with my wife.

"Jane's seven years old," I complained. "Why weren't you honest with her? Why don't you just say that the tooth fairy doesn't really exist? Why don't you admit that I'm the one who leaves the quarter for teeth?"

"Maybe you're right," she conceded. "Maybe we should be more frank and direct with the children."

The lecture really sank in.

That night at the dinner table Richard was just toying with his vegetables.

"You'd better eat them up," my wife warned. "Otherwise the little bear on the bottom of your dish will beat you to them."

I give up.

# Don't Drink the Water!

WHEN I WAS A CHILD, ONE OF THE BIG TREATS AFTER playing hard was to come home and have a glass of water.

Sometimes, if we were good, mother would even put a chip of ice in it.

However, things are different today as I found out when three young members of the Affluent Society stormed in the house and announced they were thirsty.

"Could we have some soda pop?" their spokesman asked.

"There isn't any," I informed them.

"How about some instant milk shakes?"

"Your mother hasn't gone shopping yet but they're on her list. Sorry."

"Okay, we'll have apple juice, orange juice or lemonade."

"We're out of them all," I apologized.

"But we're thirsty," they protested. "What can we drink?"

"You'll have to have water."

"What's water?"

"It's a drink."

"I thought water was something you washed your car in."

"It is, but you can drink it, too."

"Are you sure?" I was asked.

"Try some," I suggested. "You don't have to finish it if you don't like it."

They agreed and I brought in a pitcher of water with some ice.

"Don't you have to mix it with anything?"

"No."

"Does it come in any other color?"

"Not usually."

"How about flavors?"

"This is it," I had to confess.

"Will it fizz if I shake it?"

"I'm afraid not."

"Is vitamin C added?"

"No."

"Does it come in a tin, a bottle or a paper package?"

"It comes out of a tap," I said.

"Then you don't get any prizes, coupons or baseball pictures for drinking water?"

"No."

"What kind of a drink are you trying to palm off on us?"

"Try a sip before you make any decision." I begged.

They agreed.

The first member of the Affluent Society put his lips to the glass and announced, "It needs a couple of scoops of ice cream, or something."

The next took a sniff and complained, "It's flat. It doesn't have any taste."

And then he spat it out.

The third refused to go even that far. "I may be thirsty but I'm not thirsty enough to drink that icky stuff."

And they walked out.

I don't know why experts worry so much about the world running out of drinking water. Most people under the age of twenty have never tasted it anyway.

# Brownie Points

OUR JANE (WHO IS NINE) HAS JUST JOINED THE BROWNIES.

And she's enthusiastic.

She's bought the Brownie handbook; she's learned the Brownie salute; and she's dickering with a friend for a second-hand Brownie uniform.

However, the road to sainthood isn't without pitfalls, as Jane discovered this morning.

Jane's first Brownie meeting is Wednesday.

So today she was in her bedroom reciting aloud the Brownie Motto, the Brownie Promise and sundry other bits of Brownie philosophy.

*"A Smile and a Good Turn,"* she announced.

*"When helping others all the while,*
*Brownies always wear a smile;*
*When things go wrong or they fall down,*
*Brownies never . . ."*

That's as far as she got.

"Mom!" Jane bellowed. "Get Richard out of my room. He's making faces at me."

I could hear Richard (who just turned seven) giggle.

"Richard, leave your sister alone," my wife ordered.

Jane started again.

"... *Brownies never wear a frown;*
*Frowns or scowls make ugly things,*
*Smiling gives them angel wings ...*"

There was another break in the recitation.

"Richard, if you don't stop bugging me, I'll kill you," Jane threatened.

A door slammed.

"*While in the home or on the street,*
*Brownies watch each one they meet,*
*Whispering to themselves they say,*
*Is my good turn for you ...*"

The stanza was left hanging there.

"I warned you, Richard," Jane shouted, interrupting herself.

Richard came charging along the hallway and down the stairs with Jane in hot pursuit.

By the time I got to the scene, Richard was on the ground with his sister shaking him by the neck.

"I'm trying to learn my Brownie poem," Jane fumed, "and

he keeps opening my door and sticking his tongue out at me."

"Richard will leave you alone," I said. "Won't you, Richard?"

Richard couldn't talk, not with Jane's hands around his throat, but he nodded in agreement.

"If you do it again, I'll pull your tongue out," Jane vowed. Jane then let him up.

Richard decided to go over to Chippy's and play on the swing, which appeared to be a hell of a lot safer than heckling our resident Brownie.

When I left for the office, I could hear Jane in her bedroom.

*"Brownies' smiles go all the way,*
*And with them a good turn a day."*
Her right hook isn't bad either.

# Bits and Overbites

EVERYBODY HAS SOME PHYSICAL CHARACTERISTIC THAT'S embarrassing.

With my daughter Jane, it's her teeth.

When Jane smiles, she tries not to open her mouth or, if she does, she quickly covers it with her hand to hide the view.

The problem is, Jane's teeth are straight and even.

That's right, Jane doesn't have braces.

Nor does she have much hope of ever wearing braces. The family dentist says her teeth are coming in straight and, sorry, there's nothing he can do about it.

I don't have to tell you how Jane feels.

Most of her friends have enough metal in their mouths to build a Japanese sports car.

When they smile, you don't see pearls; the view is pure Stelco.

So Jane feels left out.

Orthodontia is the adolescent chic of suburbia. It's status and, according to psychologists, proves your parents care.

I've tried to explain to Jane it's nobody's fault her teeth are perfect. We all have crosses to bear and this is something she'll have to accept.

For a time my explanation worked, but now we have a new crisis on our hands.

Jane's brother Stephen has developed a list of dental problems as long as a basketball player's leg.

Stephen has overbite; he's cutting into his soft palate; he's a mouth-breather; there's a space between his front teeth.

What that adds up to is 800 bucks worth of work.

The day Stephen got his braces I could tell from the look on Jane's face we were in for trouble.

"Will Stephen have to wear braces long?" she asked.

"Two years," I admitted.

"Did he get cat whiskers, too?"

I said he did.

Jane stormed out of the room, gnashing her perfect little teeth.

The next day when Jane came home from school I saw something glistening in her mouth.

"What's that?" I asked.

"A paper clip." Jane revealed.

"A paper clip?"

"Yes, a paper clip. I straightened it out and hooked it across my teeth," Jane stated. "I'm not going to be the only one in the entire world without braces on my teeth."

# Wheeler Dealer

OUR RICHARD (WHO IS SEVEN) SAID HE WANTED TO TALK TO ME.

"Dad," he began, "would you buy me a bike?"

"You're not old enough," I informed him.

"Murray and Peter and Bruce have bikes," he argued.

"That's their parents' decision, not mine. Besides, the street is too busy for you to be riding a bike."

"I wouldn't ride on the main streets—only the quiet ones," Richard bargained. "And I'd be very careful."

"You can't ride a bike," I reminded him. "I don't want you learning . . .

"I can ride a bike," Richard interrupted. "I learned last summer on Donald's."

Realizing I was on the run, I threw a low blow.

"Look, Richard," I said, "any boy who still sucks on his blankie isn't old enough to ride a bicycle out on the street."

Immediately I felt guilty, but triumphant.

Richard is mature, reliable and able to cut his own meat— but he does whip out pieces of an old baby blanket to suck in moments of stress and at bedtime.

In fact, he has about a dozen bits of "blankie" stashed around in case of emergency.

Besides the one by his bed, he has a scrap in the glove compartment of my car, another in the sports jacket he wears to Sunday school, etc., etc.

After my bombshell, Richard looked at me.

"Would you buy me a bike if I gave up my blankie?" he wanted to know.

"Well, I suppose so," I replied.

What else could I say?

"Would you get me a real two-wheeler, with a bell?"

"Yes—if you give up your blankie," I said, emphasizing every syllable so Richard would understand what he was getting into.

"All right, I'll give up my blankie," Richard sighed. "When do I get my bike?"

"In the spring, when the nice weather arrives," I said.

"Can I pick it out myself?"

"Yes," I agreed. "Do you think you can give up your blankie?"

"I think so," Richard answered. "But Dad, would you do me a favor?"

"If I can," I promised.

"Will you hide all my blankies so I can't find them?"

# Good Deeds

I MADE A TERRIBLE MISTAKE A MONTH AGO. I LET OUR Richard join the Cubs.

Believe me, I have nothing against the Cubs. I respect their traditions and buy their apples.

But I have come to learn that no kitchen in the world is big enough to hold a Cub AND a Brownie.

As you may recall, Jane is our resident Brownie and has been since last September.

Naturally, she's come to look upon every dirty dish in the house as her own.

So long comes the upstart Cub who immediately tries to

horn in on her good deed racket.

You can imagine the result.

Every night there's a fight after supper between our Cub and our Brownie over the dishes.

Last evening, for example, Richard grabbed a dirty dinner plate from Jane's hands and said, "It's my turn to do the dishes."

"It is not." Jane replied, snatching the plate back. "You set the table for dinner. It's my turn to do a good deed."

"Oh, yeah?" Richard shot back. "You made Mom's bed this morning."

"Yes, but you fed the dog and took her for a walk after school," Jane accused. "You know I'm trying to get my pet badge."

"I only fed the dog because you vacuumed the rug in the living room", Richard answered. "That's my job. Mom said so."

"Can I help it if you were outside helping Dad stack the firewood?" our Brownie sniffed.

"Give me that dirty plate, Jane."

"Try and make me . . ."

At that point my wife interrupted. "Stop fighting or I won't let either of you do the dishes," she warned.

Faced with that ultimatum, they agreed to share the good deed.

"But don't take more than your share of dirty dishes," Jane cautioned, "or I'll tell."

"I get to wipe the table!" Richard shouted triumphantly.

Jane's face dropped a mile.

Fortunately, Stephen (who is twelve) belongs to no group and never bugs us to do a good deed. Thank heaven!

There just isn't enough dust, cutlery, dog, and firewood to keep THREE kids in badges.

# Jane's Ballet Recital

WATCHING YOUR DAUGHTER PERFORM IN HER FIRST DANCE
recital is a moving experience, especially if she has brothers.

It's a recognized fact small boys don't like (1) dancing,
(2) sitting still for longer than twelve seconds, and (3) sisters.

So an evening of dance is a challenge.

However, I was insistent.

If Jane (who is nine) could spend every Monday evening
for the past two years at ballet, the least her brothers could
do was clap.

We took our seats—me on the aisle, then Jane's mother,
Richard (who is seven) and Stephen (who is twelve).

The house lights dimmed, the music (taped) began, the
first group of little girls came on stage and . . .

"How much longer?" Richard asked in a loud whisper.

"Shhh!" I informed him behind his mother's back.

"How much longer did Dad say?" Stephen demanded of
Richard.

"Dad said, 'Shhh!' " Richard repeated.

"Shhh!" I said.

"When's Jane coming out?" Richard wanted to know as
soon as the first number was almost half over.

"Soon."

"How soon?"

"Pretty soon."

"How soon is 'pretty soon'?"

"About thirty minutes."

"Can we leave as soon as Jane . . .?"

"Why don't we switch seats so you can sit next to Richard?" my wife suggested.

We did. It was now Jane's mother on the aisle, then me, Richard and Stephen.

"Ask Dad if I can go and get a drink," Stephen blared in Richard's ear.

"Stephen wants to know . . ."

"The answer is no," I replied.

"Dad says . . ."

"I heard him," Stephen grumbled.

"Ouch!" Richard exclaimed.

"What's going on?" I asked.

"Stephen pinched me."

"I did not."

"You did so—right on the arm."

"Both of you, stop it. And Richard, sit up in that seat. What are you doing on the floor?"

"I'm looking for something."

"For what?"

"My gum. When Stephen pinched me I dropped my gum."

"Shhh!" said a voice from the row behind.

"Sit between the boys," my wife whispered.

Richard and I switched seats.

The arrangement didn't last long, however, because Richard allegedly reached behind me and gave Stephen a shot.

"We've got to keep the boys as far apart as possible," my wife finally decreed.

For the last time we all got up and changed seats—Stephen on the aisle, my wife, me, then Richard.

Like I say, watching my daughter's first dance recital was truly one of the most moving experiences of my life.


# First Bra


WHY IS IT WE CAN REMEMBER THE DARK MOMENTS OF LIFE so clearly? Every word, every detail . . .

It was the morning of June twenty-sixth, precisely at 7:30 (which is when we always get up). And the members of the family were gathered around our bed.

That's because it was Jane's tenth birthday and she was opening her gifts.

A yo-yo from Stephen. Bubble gum from Richard (his

favorite flavor, graperoo). A sleeping bag from us. Cash
from her grandparents.

And, from her grandparents in Montreal—a bra?
My God!
My little Jane! My little pigtailed Jane!
Why it seems only yesterday she
was doing double dutches in the side drive.

And it was.

At first I thought it was all a ghastly mistake. My daughter
is growing up but out is an entirely different direction.

Surely the bra was intended for Jane's mother, perhaps as
a belated anniversary present. Or . . .

But no. The tag on the bra definitely indicated it was for
Jane.

And Jane was clearly delighted even though at this stage,
the only thing in double figures is her age.

Her brothers (especially Richard) howled at the sight of
the bra and threatened to tell all their friends.

I put a stop to that.

My wife's parents may put ideas into Jane's head but
they're not going to put ideas into the heads of a lot of ten-
year-old boys, not if I can help it.

Later, Jane and I had a heart-to-heart talk and she agreed the bra was a little premature.

"I probably won't need one till I'm twelve or thirteen," she informed me.

"That's right," I responded. "Remember, your grandparents live in Montreal. Ten-year-olds mature much faster down there."

How much longer can I hold the floodgates against time? I don't know.

Two weeks ago Richard (who is seven) came into the house filthy and my wife announced she was going to give him a bath.

Richard was mortified.

He finally agreed his mother could give him a bath under one condition—that he be permitted to wear swim trunks in the tub while she was doing the scrubbing.

What's happening to my babies?


# Seven Times Eight

THE MOST DIFFICULT THING TO SWALLOW AROUND OUR house these days is supper.

No it has nothing to do with the quality of the food—my wife still cooks with the average of them.

And my appetite is sound as a yen.

So what's the problem?

My daughter Jane.

Jane is everything a father could hope for in a ten-year-old girl—tidy, polite and built straight as a stick.

However, our dream child does have a tiny flaw: mathematics.

More specifically, Jane doesn't know her times tables, especially her seven times tables.

If you want to track it down further, Jane hasn't any idea what seven times eight equals.

Jane can tell you how much Karen's father makes (with bonuses), where babies come from, who in the neighborhood wears support stockings and why the people at the corner have their house for sale.

For all I know, Jane may have the cure for the common cold tucked up the sleeve of her Charlie Brown sweatshirt.

But she doesn't know seven times eight.

So for the past week at the dinner table we've been firing math questions at Jane.

Last night, as usual, it began with the salad course.

"What's six times six?" I started.

"Thirty-six," Jane snapped back.

"What's three times eight?" her big brother demanded.

"Twenty-four," was the response.

"And five times nine?" I continued.

"Forty-five," Jane answered.

Then Jane's mother came in with the toughie. "And what's seven times eight?"

We all crossed our fingers.

"Fifty-two?" Jane suggested.

"No," we all shouted. "Fifty-six!"

"Jane, before we ruin another meal," I decreed, "I want you to write, 'Seven times eight is 56,' and I want you to write it 100 times."

This morning at breakfast I was able to see the fruits of my crash course.

"What's seven times eight?" I asked Jane.

"Fifty-six," she replied.

It was a wonderful moment.

Unfortunately, her brother spoiled it.

"What's eight times seven?" he asked.

"Fifty-two?" Jane suggested.

# You're Number One

FOR SOME STRANGE REASON THERE'S TERRIFIC RIVALRY among our children.

Sometimes it gets pretty ridiculous.

For example, the other day I caught the three of them arguing—get this—over who had the worst cold.

"My cold's worse than yours, Stephen," Jane was challenging.

"It is not," Stephen countered. "I've been sniffing and blowing my nose all day, so there."

"Well Mom says my face is flushed and I may have to stay home from school tomorrow. Nah!" Jane responded.

"Achoo!" Richard trumped.

That's when I stepped in.

"Who cares who has the worst cold?" I asked. "Is it worth fighting over? Why do you have to make comparisons all the time?"

The lecture (as the kids realized) was about to begin.

"I'm tired of listening to the three of you wrangle over who has the best this or the biggest that.

"Why do you do it—to get attention?

"You know your mother and I love you all—and equally. As far as we're concerned, you're all Number One. There is no Number Two or Number Three in this house.

"You all get the same treatment.

"So why the arguments?

"Supposing Jane's cold is the worst—and I'm just supposing. So what? Nobody will miss a meal or be forgotten just because Jane needs a little extra care.

"Next week it may be Stephen who has the cold—or Richard.

"But, in the long run, it all evens out.

"Do you understand what I'm saying?

"Don't always look around to see if your sister or brother is getting more dessert, a newer bicycle, a better math mark.

"You'll never be happy if you do that.

"Enjoy what you have—and for heaven's sake, stop competing with each other all the time."

I paused to let my words sink in.

Stephen finally broke the silence.

"I don't compete as much as Jane does," he said.

"You do so," Jane replied. "You compete more, and so does Richard."

"I do not."

"You do so . . ."

# Our Christmas Letter

INSTEAD OF CARDS, WE'RE SENDING OUT A CHRISTMAS "letter" this year. This is how it goes.

Dear . . .

With another Yuletide upon us, it's time to bring you up to date on what happened at our house this past year.

The big news was that Gary didn't get the promotion at the office he was hoping for. Nor did he write a book, sign a TV contract or win a daily double at the racetrack.

But the year wasn't a total loss for Gary. He says the eczema on his right leg is just about cleared up and, with only one infected leg, he has cut his scratching time almost in half.

I tell him at his age he's lucky to have any itch at all, ha, ha.

Stephen became a teenager this year. Yes, he turned thirteen this month and he can't wait for his voice to change.

Personally, we feel the same way about his socks.

You probably wouldn't recognize Stephen any more. That's because of the big black thing growing out of his ear. It's called a telephone and he's on it all the time.

We suspected Stephen was growing up this past summer when he asked for his first can of deodorant. Then we discovered he was using it to spray ants in his bedroom. How he could ever find their little armpits we still don't know.

Jane didn't stand at the top of her class this year, but she knows the girl who did, which is something, I suppose.

Her big news is that she made an entire meal for the family and got her Brownie cooking badge. Our big news is that the family survived. Now we all know why the Gourmet does so much Galloping.

Richard joined the YMCA on his eighth birthday and immediately signed up for a course in judo and karate.

As far as we can see, the only difference is that Richard still breaks furniture as fast as before, but now he's added grunts.

He certainly is active. And eat! Gary says Richard has the throat of a snake. If it's smaller than a garage, and dead, Richard can get it down with one gulp.

We just wish Richard's teacher would stop sending home notes telling us, "not to worry." We didn't—till we got the notes.

And that brings us to me.

Gary didn't surprise me this year with a new car, as I expected. (I'm still driving the 1966 Mini.) But I did get my fur coat remodelled. Now it's just what I've always wanted—a Persian lamb jacket that, in three years, will be old enough to vote.

I think those are the main highlights of this year so, from us and ours, to you and yours, happy holidays.

—The Lautens

P.S. We think Richard's second teeth are coming in crooked.

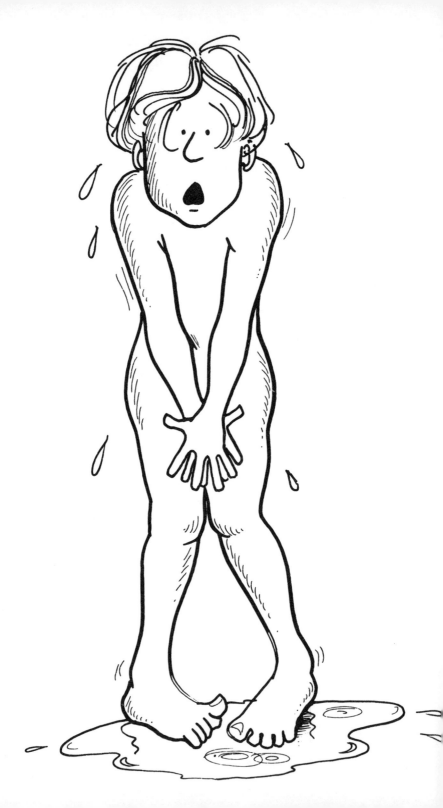

# Nude is Rude

I'VE SEEN ALL SORTS OF TOTAL STRANGERS IN THE NUDE—
Jane Fonda, Brigitte Bardot, Sally Kellerman, Jackie Onassis,
even Burt Reynolds.

But I haven't seen my own children with their clothes off,
at least not since they were babies.

Maybe a psychiatrist could explain it.

Why, when the rest of the world is parading around stark
naked in magazines, movies, on the stage, why are my kids
still hiding behind a towel?

Not only are they unwilling to accept frontal nudity, they
reject aft as well.

Take Richard.

Richard is only nine but he absolutely refuses to disrobe in
front of witnesses.

Just the other day, for example, I had to get something
from the bathroom where Richard was having a bath.

"Can I come in?" I asked through the closed door.

"I'm having a bath," Richard shouted.

"It will only take a second," I promised.

"Couldn't it wait?" he wanted to know.

"No," I said.

"Well . . ."

"Richard, let me in."

"Okay," he surrendered.

"Richard, the door is locked," I grumbled, rattling the
knob.

"Just a minute," he said.

I could hear him get out of the tub, take off the lock, and then make a mad dash back to the bath, to the foamiest corner, I'm sure.

"You can come in now," Richard announced. "But promise you won't look."

Richard's brother and sister are the same.

Richard's brother went through an entire volleyball season without once taking a shower at the school gym.

And Jane props a chair against her bedroom door even when she changes her mind.

For all I know, my children could be covered with suggestive tattoos, or have vines growing from their navels.

Frankly, I'm worried.

"Do you think it's normal for children to be so shy about their bodies?" I asked my wife last evening as we were undressing for bed.

"I can't hear you," she replied. "Can't you wait till you come out of the closet to tell me?"

# Hugs

FOR MANY YEARS, I'VE REFERRED TO MY SON RICHARD AS "MY partner, buddy and pal."

And he's responded in kind.

But lately there's been a change in our relationship, a sort of cooling off.

Specifically, Richard has been pretty stingy with his hugs lately. Sometimes I go days without one.

This is a great loss because my partner, buddy and pal dishes out neat hugs. Lots of squeeze and life.

Oh, he still likes me to scratch his back every night before he goes to bed, especially right in the middle.

However, the hugs are definitely in short supply.

This morning, I decided to broach the subject at the breakfast table.

"Richard, how come you don't hug me as often as you used to?" I asked, getting right to the point. "Aren't we still partners, buddies and pals?"

"Aw, dad," he replied, looking very embarrassed.

"Is it because you're nine and think you're too old for that kind of stuff?"

Richard didn't answer, but I could see I had hit the nail on the head.

I then launched into a defence of hugs.

"Hugs are okay, Richard, no matter how old you are. Just because you hug some one doesn't mean you're a sis.

"Why, your mother and I hug, jet pilots hug, Darryl Sittler hugs, Prime Minister Trudeau hugs, your teacher hugs—I bet even Captain Kirk hugs.

"All it means is that you like someone and that isn't wrong."

Richard didn't look up so I kept on going.

"I know you're a seconder at Cubs and you weight seventy-three pounds, and you don't need a nightlight any more, and you can stay up now until 9:30, and you can reach the top of the doorway if you stand on tiptoe.

"I know those things, Richard.

"But I'm forty-five and I need hugs. I especially need them at the end of a tough day when the world seems to be going nuts.

"So how about it?

"Can't you spare one hug a day? Not a crummy little hug. I mean the real thing so I can wrap my arms around you for a minute or two."

Richard finally looked into my face.

"Okay, Dad." he surrendered.

And then he added, "But not in front of my friends, okay?"

Obviously Richard is growing up and, I guess, so am I. It's rotten.

# You Know What? *What?*

OUR RICHARD MUST THINK I'M THE MOST STUPID MAN IN the entire world.

Every day he asks me the same question about 135 times—and I never have the answer.

The question is, "You know what, Dad?"

Richard uses it to start, carry on and finish all of his conversations.

He repeats the phrase so often I'm not sure if he's my son or my Sony.

Yesterday, for example, Richard broke into the house just bursting with good news.

"You know what, Dad?" he began.

"No, what," I replied.

"George and Peter and Michael and me have a new club, and you know what?"

"What?"

"We're building a neat clubhouse down the creek, out of wood, and you know what?"

"What?"

"We're going to make money by collecting bottles and papers and doing jobs around the house, and you know what?"

"What?"

"We're calling our club The Rats and I'm president, and you know what?"

"What?"

"Jane wants to join our club because we have a neat crest and a clubhouse and everything but she's a girl, and you know what?"

"What?"

"Girls aren't allowed to join the Rats, and you know what?"

It was at that point I surrendered.

As gently as possible, I explained to Richard that he should tell the story without interruptions.

"It's your story," I reminded. "And I'm dying to hear it.

"But can't you tell me without asking if I know what?"

"Richard, I don't know what. I don't expect to know what in the future. And, if I ever knew what in the past, I've forgotten now.

"So just tell me about The Rats and the clubhouse and Jane."

Richard was ready to continue with his story when I reminded him one more time.

"Remember," I said, "I don't know what."

"Well, Dad," Richard responded eagerly, "guess what?"

"What?" I said.

# Flu Facts

IF YOU'RE A MOTHER, THESE THINGS ARE GUARANTEED TO happen when one of your children gets the flu . . .

The little one will wake you at three o'clock in the morning, breathe all over your face, and announce: "I think I'm going to be sick."

The flu victim will then dash for the bathroom—and not quite make it.

Your husband will sleep through the incident.

When you call the doctor in the morning, he won't be in; his nurse will be busy; but the girl on the switchboard will tell you there's a lot of it going around and she'll send over a prescription.

The messenger from the drug store will want $9.75, and not have change for a $10 bill.

The brothers of the flu victim will complain because the flu victim has the small TV in her bedroom, is getting all the ginger ale she wants, and doesn't have to go to school.

The flu victim will have barely enough strength to shout, "Mom!" seventy-eight times during your favorite daytime TV serial.

The family dog will spend the entire day on the flu victim's bed, taking turns licking the flu victim's popsicle.

The $9.75 prescription will upset the flu victim's stomach and it will cause the flu victim to throw up all over her bed.

Classmates will send the flu victim a get-well card.

The get-well card will be ten feet long and the flu victim will cry until you drop everything and paste it up on her bedroom wall.

When you're halfway up the stairs, the telephone will ring; it will be your husband asking how the flu victim is feeling.

The flu victim's brothers will ask if they can have the flu victim's bike if she dies.

The flu victim's temperature will peak (101.5) about a half hour before you're supposed to leave for the dinner party you've been looking forward to all week.

You'll have a domestic scene when your husband brings home a large chocolate bar, with nuts, as a special treat for the flu victim.

Your husband will say, no, he won't clean it up if anything happens.

The flu victim will say she's feeling a lot better, and can

she, please, come downstairs and watch television with the rest of the family.

The flu victim, after a week at home, will go back to school.

You'll breathe a sigh of relief.

At three o'clock in the morning, the flu victim's brother will wake up, breathe all over your face and announce: "I think I'm going to be sick."

CAN I HAVE YOUR BIKE IF YOU DIE?

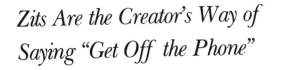

# Zits Are the Creator's Way of Saying "Get Off the Phone"

# A Difficult Stage

I'M GOING THROUGH A VERY DIFFICULT STAGE IN LIFE—MY son's teens. I've been affected in dozens of ways.

For example, before Stephen turned thirteen and entered high school, I spoke normally; my pitch was steady, my tone firm.

Now my voice is changing.

It goes up and down a hundred times a day, especially during the dinner hour which Stephen spends on the telephone talking to his friends.

Stephen only has to ask why he can't drop French seventy-five to eighty times and my voice cracks all over the place.

Yesterday, while discussing why I didn't want him to blow up the basement with his chemical set, my voice hit a note high enough to shatter a beer mug.

In short, when I open my mouth these days, even I'm surprised at what comes out.

Stephen's teens have also ruined my complexion.

Just a few short months ago my skin was the envy of the office. It may sound immodest, but my cheeks were probably in the top ten in Metro Toronto.

Now I've got a hive as big as a dollar (a paper dollar) on my forehead.

It's from watching Stephen eat, and eat, and eat. Frankly, I'm worried I can't afford it. I have the terrible feeling he's digging my grave (pauper's) with his teeth.

Another thing I've discovered since Stephen turned thirteen is that I've become terribly insecure about sex.

When Stephen was little, I had no hesitation about catching his mother as she bent over the dinner table and giving her a pat on the shoulder.

Not any more.

Stephen has taken all sorts of courses on family life and now I'm sure he can spot a fondle a mile away.

So I keep my hands to myself. If he finds out patting girls on the shoulder is loads of fun, it won't be from me.

Shy?

I don't know how to act around his friends any more. They don't seem interested in talking about beef prices or how many miles to the gallon I'm getting on the Vega.

And they're too big to offer a cookie while they wait for Stephen.

Fortunately, I'm not going through this difficult time in my life alone.

Stephen realizes the teen years are difficult ones for a father so he is being extra patient.

Just the other day he gave me this comforting thought, "I won't be a teenager forever, Dad."

Thank God he's understanding.

# For Your Ears Only

MY WIFE CALLED ME ASIDE A FEW DAYS AGO AND WHISPERED
the words that have caused fathers to weep since time began.

"Your daughter wants her ears pierced," she said.

"You mean our little Jane who only yesterday was skipping
rope in the driveway, carrying around a rag doll wherever
she went, and learning to tie her own shoelaces?" I gasped.

"That's the one," my wife answered. "What do you think?"

"But she's only a child," I protested. "It can't be more
than a year ago—two at most—that I changed her diapers,
walked her after her two a.m. feeding, burped her over my
shoulder . . ."

"Jane is twelve years old and you never did those things.
That was my job."

"That's beside the point," I insisted. "Jane's too young to
have her ears pierced."

"Her friend, Karen, has her ears pierced."

"Pierced ears are just the beginning," I warned. "Next
come the tattered jeans, music blaring from some top forty
radio station, dates with boys with long necks and spotty
complexions, a subscription to _Cosmopolitan_, green eye
shadow—God, there's no telling where it will end!"

"All she wants is to pierce her ears. My ears are pierced,
you know."

"Sure, but you were twenty and married when you had it
done. At twenty, you're mature enough to handle stud,
dangly, even hoop earrings. But Jane just got out of
Brownies.

"Can you imagine what would happen if she got into a fight with one of her brothers and they got a finger in one of her earrings? They'd stretch her ear lobe down to her waist," I said. "Or else they'd snap it until she got dizzy."

"I think you're right," my wife replied.

"You do?"

"Yes, but I wanted to make sure how you felt before Jane talked to you. She's waiting outside now."

"Why do I have to tell her?"

"Because you're her father and you feel strongly about a twelve-year-old getting her ears pierced."

"Okay, tell Jane to come in," I said, "and leave us alone."

After a twenty-minute talk with Jane, I emerged with the announcement, "I've got some good news and some bad news."

"What's the bad news?" my wife asked.

"After hearing how much it means to Jane, I've agreed she can get her ears pierced."

"What's the good news?"

"In return, Jane has given me her word she won't get married until she's at least thirteen."

I always was a hard bargainer.

# How You Get Zits

OUR JANE IS THIRTEEN AND ALL SHE WANTS FROM LIFE AT this time is a good complexion. Every morning she examines her face for blemishes, or zits, as her friends call them.

Just the other day she asked me how a person gets zits and, naturally, I didn't lose the opportunity to make a few points.

This, I told Jane, is what causes a bad complexion:

1. Listening to Elton John records at full volume while father is trying to read the paper, nap, or breathe.

2. Sitting on cold benches at the shopping plaza.

3. Leaving the house in the morning without making your bed.

4. Karate-chopping a person of the opposite sex, like a brother, across the throat while he is eating a grilled cheese sandwhich at the kitchen table.

5. Neglecting math homework.

6. Being on the telephone more than twelve times in any one-hour period.

7. Wearing eye shadow.

8. Not walking the dog when it's your turn.

9. Allowing a person selling religious tracts into the house and saying that your parents are home and you'll get them.

10. Locking yourself in the bathroom for twenty minutes in the morning when your father is in a hurry to get to work.

11. Riding on the back of a moped with anybody, but especially if he has metal studs in his clothes and wears a T-shirt that has rude words printed on the front.

12. Having more than fifteen friends in your bedroom at one time.

13. Not calling at four o'clock to say where you are.

14. Tight jeans.

15. Tight anything else.

16. Sleeping in past eleven o'clock on Saturday morning.

17. Riding a ten-speed bike that cost 100 bucks over curbs.

18. Getting up from the dinner table and not taking the dirty dishes over to the sink, rinsing them off, and then loading the dishwasher.

19. Asking more than fifteen times why you can't stay up and watch the midnight horror movie with Kim.

20. Bursting into your parents' bedroom without knocking.

21. Changing underwear, nail polish, "best" girl friend or

locker partner more than three times a day.

22. Popping the retainer in and out of your mouth while other people are eating.

23. Hitting a tennis ball against the side of the house.

24. Not putting things back where they belong.

25. And finally, eating greasy food.

Needless to say, I expect to come up with other causes of bad complexion in the days ahead, but this, at least, is a start.

# Rah Deal

OUR STEPHEN CAME HOME EARLY FROM SCHOOL YESTERDAY and of course his mother wanted to know what was wrong.

"Nothing," he said. "They're having a rally in the gym for the game tonight so I came home."

"Why didn't you stay?" his mother asked.

"Aw, Mom," he replied, screwing up his face in disgust.

Stephen considers pep rallies uncool, like wearing a hat, kissing relatives and taking public transportation, and his mother knows it.

"You should have more school spirit," his mother persisted.

Perhaps I should explain that Stephen's mother was one of those people who went through high school with a letter stencilled on the seat of her knickers.

In fact, if it hadn't been for my wife, when the Saltfleet High cheerleaders turned their backs to the crowd and bent over, they would have spelled S-L-T-F-L-E-E-T. Her "A" made all the difference.

Stephen, however, is unimpressed.

"Mom, I'm not going to hang around the school yelling my head off like a loony."

That was too much for my wife. She knelt on one knee and started to go through the old Saltfleet locomotive: *"Give me an S, give me an A, give me an L, give me a T . . ."*

"Mom, stop!" Stephen begged.

*". . . give me an F, give me an L, give me an E . . ."*

"Mom, people will see you!"

*". . . give me an E, give me a T—Saltfleet! Saltfleet! Rah, rah, rah!"*

Stephen groaned and buried his head under a chesterfield cushion, but his mother wasn't finished.

*"Blue, white, gold; blue, white, gold; they're the colors we uphold; hit 'em high, hit 'em low; Saltfleet, Saltfleet, go, go, go!"*

"Stop, please!" Stephen pleaded, mortified beyond description.

"We're not rough, we're not tough, but, boy, are we determined!" his mother shouted, putting on her cute-as-a-button smile and gazing into a non-existent grandstand.

"Mom!" our teenaged son yelled. "Don't!"

Mom, however, kept sss-boom-bah-ing and phi-ki-sighing up and down the living room floor.

"Themistocles, Thermopylae, the Peloponnesian War; X-squared, Y-squared, $H_2SO_4$; the French verbs, the Latin verbs, Archimedes' Law . . ."

In desperation, Stephen turned to me and with a look of helplessness in his eyes said, "Dad, can't you say something to Mom?"

"Cartwheels!" I bellowed. "How about a cartwheel?"

Poor Stephen. Next pep rally he'll stay at school, where its comparatively quiet.

# Father of the Babysitter

LIFE HAS CAST ME IN A NEW ROLE—THAT OF FATHER OF THE babysitter.

Believe me, looking for a babysitter (a job I had for years) is easier than having one right in your own home.

Our Jane got a call from a couple seeking her services as a babysitter after one of Jane's friends had recommended her.

Well, Jane is thirteen, responsible, and a graduate of the neighborhood YMCA's babysitting course.

But, up till then, she had never babysat anyone but her younger brother. That is, she had babysat, but not for cash money.

So Jane's mother and I were a little nervous about her first babysitting job.

"What do we know about this couple?" Jane's mother asked. "Are they decent, reliable people? After all they do live almost four blocks away."

Jane admitted she had never met her prospective employers, but her friend Tammie said they were wonderful people.

Tammie, I pointed out, also approves of Elton John, and I wouldn't want my daughter spending the evening in his pad.

Anyway, the deal was made and Jane agreed to babysit last Saturday evening after a promise from her employers that they wouldn't be late. (As Jane's Al Eagleson, I felt that was an important point to include in her contract.)

When the car pulled into the driveway to pick up Jane, all members of our family raced to the picture window.

"Get the license number of the car," I ordered Jane's older brother as I smiled through the window at the fellow behind the wheel. "And take down the guy's description, too."

Jane's brother nodded, and did as he was told.

"What do you think of him?" I asked Jane's mother as we both waved, still smiling, at our daughter as she got into the car.

"At least he isn't wearing a black cape," Jane's mother replied, showing all sorts of teeth at the stranger.

"Isn't there someone in the back seat?" I demanded, beaming my warmest grin at my daughter's first babysitting customer.

"Yes, it looks like two little girls," Jane's mother shot back. "They must be the children she's babysitting."

"That's a good sign," I replied as the car backed out and drove away, and I made a mental note of the car's color and the luggage rack on top.

Of course we stayed home ourselves, near the telephone. We wanted to be available if Jane needed us. After all, one of her charges could swallow something, or refuse to go to bed.

Shortly after eleven o'clock, the same car drove up to our

house and Jane got out.

All of us lined up by the window again, smiled some more—and then whipped to the door to greet Jane.

"How did it go?" I asked.

Jane said it was fine. She didn't have any trouble, she made $3.25 and (in response to my question) no, she didn't smell anything on the man's breath.

In short, Jane enjoyed it.

It appears I'm destined to spend a lot of my Saturday nights smiling through my picture window, taking down license numbers, and staying home.

# Frown at the Birdie

THE FASTEST WAY TO WIPE THE SMILE OFF A BOY'S FACE IS to take his picture.

Our Richard has just brought home his class photograph and, wouldn't you know it, there he is in the back corner, looking (again) like an escapee from Kingston Pen.

He's wearing a tatty jean-jacket, a T-shirt that appears to be a veteran of 345 performances with a road company of *A Streetcar Named Desire*, and a scowl that could sour powdered cream.

In short, any casual observer would get the impression that this is a kid who'd steal rubber tips from the canes of little old ladies.

But how can I complain? Every other boy in the picture looks exactly the same.

At a rough guess I'd say the boys' rows in the photograph represent at least $15,000 in orthodontics, but not one of the little fellows is showing so much as a tooth, let alone an entire corrected overbite.

If I didn't know better, I'd say they had been taking glowering lessons and were under orders not to smile on threat of death.

Meanwhile, in the other two rows of the class photograph we have sixteen winsome, bright, cheerful, sunny little girls, each one looking as if she had just stepped out of a Jello ad.

Hair brushed, dresses pressed, smiles in place, they exude sweetness, charm and cleanliness.

What is it about a Kodak that turns little girls into angels, and does everything but put a number under the faces of their male classmates?

Our Richard is in grade six, so this is his seventh class photograph and in each one he could pass the screen test if Hollywood was looking for someone to play John Dillinger.

And our Jane (who is in grade eight) has never been snapped from a bad angle, or caught with anything but laugh lines around her eyes.

Having lived with both since day one, I know the truth of the matter in each case is somewhere in the middle.

There are days when Jane can deliver a vicious knee to the small of the back with the best of them and Richard has been known to break out in a warm grin at the breakfast table (Jane doesn't usually talk till noon), and even change his underwear without being told.

But you'd never guess it from their class pictures.

Instead of pouring millions into research to develop pictures in sixty seconds, give us brighter colors, and make it possible to take photographs in the dark, it would be wonderful if the camera industry would concentrate its efforts on turning out a lens that doesn't make every little boy look like a hood on the lam.

Just once I'd like a picture of our Richard I didn't have to hide in the dresser drawer.

# Jane Bares Some

EXCUSE ME IF I LOOK PALE. I'VE JUST SEEN OUR JANE'S graduation dress. It's stunning, chic, glamorous—and those are just a few of the things wrong with it.

Believe me, I realize Jane is almost fourteen (next month) and that a person doesn't graduate from public school every day and get her final report card at a buffet-dance.

But bare shoulders?

Mind you, I've only seen the first fitting and Jane's mother still has some sewing to do, but I've been informed a higher neckline isn't scheduled.

Of course I realize this is 1976, and Jane is growing up, but why can't Jane and her mother realize that a daughter's first formal is a big moment in a father's life?

I'm not sure if I'm ready to accept a halter top, decolletage, and a gown that shows my Jane's shoulder blades.

I was rather hoping for some prim bit of business with long sleeves, a turtleneck, and a loose-fitting top, something you could wear to a Sunday school rally or a Brownie picnic.

But this number makes Jane look, let me say it right out— attractive.

It's got a fitted waist, these awfully tiny shoulder straps, and a design at the front that could have come from France, for all I know.

I've even been informed (because I asked) that Jane doesn't intend to wear a T-shirt or blouse underneath. Where there's no dress, there'll be Jane!

Why couldn't Jane and her mother have broken the news to me gently, shown me something first that exposed Jane's elbow, or perhaps even a flash of her Adam's apple.

But to go from blue jeans and a Snoopy sweatshirt to this in one giant leap is too much.

Believe me, I'm no old silly who wants his little girl to stay a little girl. Of course I want her to grow up and wear pull-overs and one-piece bathing suits, but not just yet.

After all, Jane is still, well, a little girl.

Didn't she bury a tiny bird in the backyard last week with a carefully printed tombstone that read, "Here lies the body of a little bird that never got a chance to fly. God bless him."

Does that sound like a person who should be going to her

public school graduation in a formal that shows her shoulders?

I mean, she should still be skipping in the side drive, and asking me to tuck her in at night, and making leaf charts, and begging for a few more paragraphs of *Cinderella* before turning out the light, and asking for pony rides on Sunday afternoon, and wiggling baby teeth for my benefit at the dinner table, and . . .

How can it be that my little Jane is wearing formal dresses, and going to her first real dance, and talking about somebody named Wayne or Donald, or some such?

How can it be that fourteen years (next month) have gone so fast?

# No Can Do

IT'S A SAD DAY WHEN A FATHER IS UNMASKED TO HIS daughter as a mere mortal and not some sort of superhero who can make all her dreams come true with a snap of the old fingers.

Up till now I've been able to preserve the image with our Jane.

No noise in the basement, snowboot zipper, ketchup bottle top, rough friend, nor dreamy outfit was beyond my ability to investigate, open, unscrew, reprimand, or provide. Galahad was my middle name, and the pedestal my address.

Ha!

One word from my Feather (as I called her for years) and I would fly into action with my unbelievable courage, strength, cheque book, etc. And her problem would be solved, or at least glossed over.

However, I am undone.

Jane has come up with a request which even this devoted slave cannot answer.

Well, it isn't exactly a request but the other day I asked Jane: If she could have anything in the world she wanted, what would she ask for?

Without blinking so much as an eye (blue), Jane, who is

only a few months short of her fifteenth birthday, replied, "Hips."

"But you've got hips," I pointed out.

"I mean, you know, real hips," Jane responded.

Alas, Daddy does know. Jane wants to be stacked, built, to have the kind of figure that causes truck drivers to pile their semis into telephone poles, and think it was worth it.

Sob! Yes, my little Jane wants all of that.

Personally, I'm opposed; in truth, if I had my way, I'd cut out a couple of curves Jane already has. The last thing a father needs is a knockout daughter.

If Jane wants hips today, what will it be tomorrow—a waist, creamy shoulders, for heaven's sake, terrific thighs? Where will it end—and, please, don't answer that.

How simple it was in the old days to be Jane's hero. All it required was a maplenut cone, a boost up to the water fountain, the skill required to untangle a shoelace, the answer to seven times eight.

But hips?

What happened to my little girl who only wanted me to find the eyes to her doll, and stick them back in? Where is the child who only asked to have her brother's face removed from her elbow?

I may be a little longer in the tooth but I can still give a horsey ride on my foot, cross my eyes (always a hit in the past), provide change for the bubble-gum machine, or sit through a Walt Disney movie featuring a dog that talks, performs nuclear experiments, or reads minds.

Is all that talent to go to waste now?

Can't I bring down the house any more by pretending the din-din on the spoon is an airplane? Has my daughter lost interest in looking up my nose when we have company? Is it no longer enough to pull out a sleigh from behind the back as a surprise, or a Snoopy barrette from an inside overcoat pocket?

Hips?

I get the impression that this Daddy has just fallen flat on his abracadabra.

Well, Olympus was nice while it lasted.

# Will People Talk?

I NEVER THOUGHT I'D LIVE TO SEE THE DAY WHEN A LITTLE thing like a kiss from a gorgeous female, delivered in broad daylight in front of a few hundred witnesses, would leave me blushing and giggly.

But that is exactly what happened the other morning on a busy downtown street corner in the middle of the rush hour.

What is significant is that the kiss was planted on my cheek by my daughter, Jane.

Ordinarily I can take a smacker from family without so much as a blink, but Jane has become quite a looker this past year.

(Can you imagine the coincidence? My two sons are the best-looking boys in the world, and my daughter has a clear lead among females. Surely that's something for the *Guinness Book of Records*.)

In any case, Jane and I were walking down the street and, when it came time to make a left to school, instead of the usual wave and "See ya," Jane gave me the embrace.

Mind you, it was my birthday.

But Jane was just in mid-pucker when the thought entered my mind: Will the people witnessing this scene realize Jane is my daughter, and I'm her father, and, well, it isn't one of those May-December things?

When Jane was just a kid (approximately six months ago) I

could have thrown myself into the peck with gusto. Other than the concern about whether Jane might be eating licorice and leave a mark on my face, or get bubble gum on an eyebrow, I had no deep worry.

However, Jane is about as tall as her mother now, has a dimple guaranteed to drive men wild, and possesses the good legs that are a tradition in our family, even among the women.

Why, just the other day Jane's mother reported our daughter got "two toots and a woo" on the way home from school, the toots being saucy blasts from horns (a panel truck and a moped) and the "woo" being the comment of a motorist waiting for a traffic light to change.

So you see it's not just the biased report of a proud father, although I spotted her good looks even that first day in the nursery when she was sucking the back of her hand, and needed changing.

However, that is all past. What about my role in the future as Jane's father?

In a dim light, and at a distance, if I haven't had too difficult a day at the office, I could easily pass for eighty-five or eighty-six.

Should a man looking that age risk his reputation and accept kisses on the forehead from a young doll who reads *Sixteen* magazine, no longer has feet in her pyjamas, and gets toots and woos on the way home from high school?

Should he put his arm around this young dish when they cross an intersection, share a joke in a department store, carry the family capon home from market Saturday morning, or do a dozen other things together?

Well, should he?

Yes.

My days as the Number One man in Jane's life are numbered, and I'm going to enjoy them while I can.

# A Twelve-Year-Old Boy Is . . .

MANY OF US HAVE, WERE, OR KNOW, A TWELVE-YEAR-OLD
boy. In case you've forgotten what a twelve-year-old boy is
like, let me refresh your memory.

A twelve-year-old boy forgets to bring home innoculation
notices from school.

A twelve-year-old boy never gives his sister enough room
in the back seat of the car.

A twelve-year-old boy is a master at moving his lips during
music class at school, and during hymns at church, and never
making a sound.

A twelve-year-old boy wants his mother to buy a certain

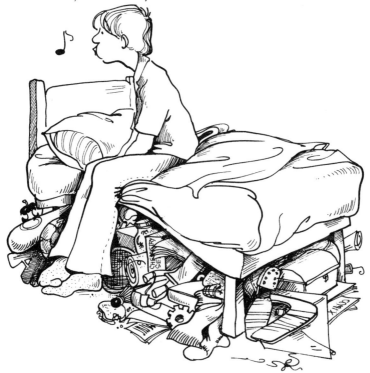

kind of cereal because there's a plastic rocket launcher inside.

A twelve-year-old boy doesn't like to eat the cereal that comes with the plastic rocket launcher.

A twelve-year-old boy doesn't like it when somebody thinks it's his sister talking on the telephone.

A twelve-year-old boy goes to his first school dance, and then climbs up the basketball backboard to get away from the girls.

A twelve-year-old boy cleans up his room by stuffing everything under his bed.

A twelve-year-old boy always has a friend whose mother lets him keep gerbils in a cardboard box in the basement.

A twelve-year-old boy never wants to grow up and be an accountant.

A twelve-year-old boy hangs around his big brother's friends whenever they'll let him.

A twelve-year-old boy cannot read without putting his feet up on the back of the chesterfield.

A twelve-year-old boy, when asked why his teacher wants to see his mother or father, replies, "Beats me."

A twelve-year-old boy has feet that sweat a lot.

A twelve-year-old boy can bruise your forehead, step on your foot, knock over an end table, and spill your coffee just while giving you a goodnight kiss.

A twelve-year-old boy hates it when the Bionic Man embraces a woman, or any of that other mush.

A twelve-year-old boy won't wear the sweater Aunt Maude sent him.

A twelve-year-old boy asks for the comic section first so he can read Spiderman.

A twelve-year-old boy would just as soon not discuss the Life Course he's taking at school from the health teacher.

A twelve-year-old boy insists he didn't have anything to eat after four at his friend's house.

A twelve-year-old boy thinks it's dumb to wash any part of him that doesn't show.

A twelve-year-old boy always leaves just enough milk in the pitcher so somebody else has to get up and refill it.

A twelve-year-old boy likes to look at himself in the mirror, and make faces, when he's sure nobody else is watching.

A twelve-year-old boy rolls up his art work in a ball and brings it home in his hat.

A twelve-year-old boy doesn't understand all the fuss about race, religion and that stuff.

A twelve-year-old boy always orders the green ice cream with the brown bits.

A twelve-year-old boy takes French because his parents say he has to.

A twelve-year-old boy sometimes, if you're lucky, will let you give him a hug, provided nobody's looking.

A twelve-year-old boy is pretty special.

# Hair Today, Gone Tomorrow

THERE ARE ALL SORTS OF LANDMARKS IN YOUR SON'S LIFE—his first words, his first faltering steps, his first tinkle in the proper facilities, his first day at school, his first ride (without help) on a two-wheeler, his first night away from home.

Well, our Stephen (who is seventeen) has reached another important first: His first moustache.

Several weeks ago he announced his intention to grow what we used to call a cookie duster.

Something neat and aristocratic in the David Niven tradition, not one of those long, flowing jobs that look as if they need a quick run-through with the Lawn Boy.

Of course his parents were crushed.

Our little tot with a moustache? It seems only yesterday we were asking him to stick out his tongue and lick the hankie so we could take the smudge off his face before meeting Grandma.

Stephen, the little mischief who, when walking down the street, would suddenly relax, hang between Mommy and Daddy's hands, and demand a swing?

Yes, that's Stephen.

(Come to think of it, it was Stephen's brother, Richard, who liked to drop like a rock and pull your shoulder out of its socket when you least expected it, but I don't want to go back and rub out that second-to-last paragraph.)

However, we took the news bravely and said whatever Stephen wanted to put on his lip was okay with us just as long as I didn't have to feed it, and his mother did not have to vacuum it Saturdays.

After assuring us on both counts, Stephen then proceeded to grow his moustache, sort of.

After skipping the area in question with his Remington for a couple of days, Stephen asked if we could see any sign of a luxurious growth sprouting up.

Frankly, he had a better moustache the last time we had grape drink, but we did not want to dash his hopes so we said the bristles were clearly visible when he stood in the light a certain way, and called him Santa Claus.

Each morning we went through the same ritual and his mother went so far as to say "ouch!" when he kissed her on his way to school, and suggested she may have been scratched by his stubble, which pleased him enormously.

Deep in my heart, though, I knew Stephen's dream was doomed. He has my complexion and coloring, and I couldn't grow enough hair on my lip to make a toupee for a gnat.

We're just not the hairy kind, a characteristic that made my mother very proud and caused her to hint that anyone so smooth of cheek must have royal blood somewhere in his veins. Kings, apparently, only have to shave every other day.

Undoubtedly you've guessed the end of this rather sad story.

Apparently Stephen finally saw the hopelessness of his cause because yesterday at breakfast he informed his loved ones, plus his brother and sister, "I've decided to shave off my moustache."

With all of the compassion at her command, his mother asked, "When are you going to do it?"

"I did it two days ago," Stephen said accusingly.

Apparently that last "ouch!" wasn't necessary.

# Dating Rules

THE MOST PRESSING QUESTION ON OUR JANE'S MIND IS: When will she be old enough to date? Our daughter will be 15 in a few weeks and wants to know.

To answer her question, I've drawn up a little table.

The age Jane can date is . . .

If the guy rides a Harley, wears an SS helmet, leather boots and jeans that have not been washed since 1973, and has a disgusting tatoo on his arm: 87.

If he carries a package of ciggies in the sleeve of his T-shirt and considers *Shirley And Laverne* an intellectual experience: 78.

If he's a member of a political party dedicated to the overthrow of the government, and makes bombs in his basement for a hobby: 71.

If he has a van with "Don't laugh, mister, your daughter may be inside" painted on the side, with more than two words misspelled: 64.

If he plays his transistor on the beach or in the park loud enough to be heard by people with serious hearing problems, and low-flying pleasure craft: 57.

If he has more than twenty-eight pounds of hair: 51.

If he has shaved his head like Kojak: 50½.

If he belongs to a religion that requires the sacrificing of goats in the mountains, painting your face blue, or dancing on a street corner while playing a saxophone: 45.

If he talks out loud in movies, rattles his popcorn bag, makes rude remarks during the love scenes, and slouches in his seat during the playing of O Canada: 41.

If he gave his mother a litre bottle of Baby Platypus last Mother's Day, and a set of blue plastic wine glasses: 39.

If he wears more cologne than his date: 37.

If he considers it a big night out to go downtown and look at the window displays of revolvers, rifles, war surplus machine guns, grenades, etc., or just make skid marks in the nearest school yard with his VW: 32.

If it's his dream to grow up and one day open a string of body rub parlors: 31.

If he got less than four on his last algebra exam: 29.

If the picture he gives his girl friend for their wallet has a number at the bottom, and includes both a front and side view: 28.

If he makes derogatory remarks about Australians: 27.

If he picks up the family pet, Sarah, by the neck, tail, or the hair in the armpits, and says it doesn't hurt her: 25.

If he wears earrings, or cheers for the Toronto Argos: 22.

If his hockey teammates call him "Animal," and the coach only lets him on the ice when the score is 7-1, either way: 21.

If he knows more than 47 waiters in the downtown area by first name, or is referred to as "Cold Hands" by more than 11 topless barmaids: 19.

If he breaks out laughing when his date's father talks about how difficult things were when he was young, and how he used to walk twelve miles to school and back: 18.

Finally, Jane can date at fifteen—IF the boy's name is Prince Andrew, and I have a talk with his mum and dad first to make sure he comes from a nice family.

What could be fairer than that?

# Suits Me to a "T"

OUR JANE IS AT THE AGE (FIFTEEN) WHEN SHE CONSIDERS herself mature enough to wear a T-shirt with printing on it.

Daddy is not so sure.

Most of the slogans I've read on T-shirts I wouldn't want plastered across my daughter's chest. They have far too much, well, tang.

However, I am not an unreasonable man.

I've told Jane she can wear a T-shirt, provided she clears its message first with me.

Is that unfair?

Of course not.

In fact, here's a rather lengthy list of slogans I've already approved for Jane's T-shirts:

**Born To Be Home By 10 o'clock
10:30 At The Latest**

**Cocoa Power**

**No, Non, Nyet And Nein**

**My Father Has A Black Belt
And A Vicious Temper**

**If You Can Read This
You're Much Too Close**

Our Family Dog, Thor, Thinks
   Strangers Are Delicious

No, We've Never Met

The Waltz Is A Lovely Dance,
   Don't You Agree?

Vatican City Beach

My Cousin's In The RCMP,
   What's Yours Do?

Don't Read This

A Knee Delivered To The Pit
   Of A Smart Aleck's Stomach
     Can Hurt Awfully

Animal's Sister

My Scream Can Be Heard
   For Over Two Miles

Yes, I Can Date
   But First You Have To Ask
     My Daddy, Clark Kent

Did You Know Kissing Can
   Cause Concussion?

My Godfather's Name Is Vito

Mormon Tabernacle Choir

If You Want A Good Time,
   Don't Call Me

Is Your OHIP Paid Up?

Little Sisters Of Charity
   Motorcycle Club

No Foolin'

One, Two, Three Strikes—
   You're Out

**Philadelphia Flyers'**
 **Ladies Auxiliary**

**No Speak Romance**

**I Sell Life Insurance**

**This T-shirt Is Equipped**
 **With A Burglar Alarm**

**If You're Planning A Wild Party**
 **Phone 967-2222**

There you have it—about thirty slogans I'd be willing to have printed on our Jane's T-shirts. Surely she can find one to her liking.

By the way, that phone number is for the Toronto Police Department. I hope the sergeant on duty won't mind taking Jane's calls.


# Richard Speaks!

OUR RICHARD IS THIRTEEN AND I'VE COME TO A LANDMARK decision: He's now old enough to talk directly to clerks in stores.

As any parent will immediately realize, it's another watershed in our lives.

Up till last Saturday, the "baby" in our family always conversed with salespersons through his mother or father.

Of course there's nothing wrong with his voice and he does have a tongue.

But traditionally that's how it's done. In the presence of a parent, children and clerks never speak to each other.

On the weekend, however, I took Richard to the neighborhood department store for a pair of slippers: We went straight to the shoe section.

"Yes?" the clerk asked.

"My son needs a pair of slippers," I informed the clerk.

"What size?" he asked me.

"What size do you take?" I asked Richard, who was standing right beside me.

"I think about an eight," Richard stated.

I looked at the clerk "About an eight."

"What color slipper would you like?" was his next question.

"What color, Richard?" I inquired.

"Blue," Richard answered smartly.

"Blue," I told the clerk.

"Any particular style?" the clerk asked me.

"Any particular style?" I demanded of my son.

"No, just as long as they don't have slippery soles and won't mark the floor," Richard said.

"No," I responded to the clerk, "just as long as they don't have slippery soles and won't mark the floor."

The clerk nodded and went into the back room, returning in a moment or two with several boxes of slippers. He slipped one on Richard's foot.

"How is that for fit?" he asked.

"How is that for fit?" I relayed to Richard.

"It's a little tight," Richard commented.

"It's a little tight," I informed the salesman.

The clerk slipped it off. "Will he be wearing socks with the slippers? Those are pretty heavy socks he has on," he commented.

"Will you be wearing socks with the slippers? Those are pretty heavy socks you have on," I passed on to Richard.

"I like heavy socks," Richard stated.

"He likes heavy socks," I repeated.

"We'll try a half-size larger," the clerk suggested. "How's this?" he asked me after putting on Richard's foot.

"How's . . ."

I broke in mid-sentence. I looked at Richard—128 pounds, taller than his mother at five feet, six inches—and I made the breakthrough.

"Richard, you tell the clerk," I said. "You two can talk to each other."

Richard was taken aback but he looked at the clerk and said, "Fine."

"Better try the other one," the clerk advised Richard directly.

Within five minutes it was all over, and it didn't sound as if the sale were taking place in an echo chamber.

It's the end of an era, I guess.

Next time we're at a restaurant, I'll even have to let Richard give his own order to the waiter. That's the ultimate.

I just hope he takes the hint if, when he orders the $12.95 filet, he feels a kick under the table.

# Fathers Knows Second Best

EVERY OCCUPATION SEEMS MORE COMPLICATED THESE DAYS, but no job has increased in difficulty more than that of father.

A few years ago a dad had to teach his son how to catch a ball, make a wooden sword from two sticks, tie a tie, and keep his head in so he didn't fall out a car window on the way to Niagara Falls.

That was about it.

Thanks to the tremendous advances made in the male lifestyle, that has all changed.

This morning, for example, Stephen (who is eighteen)

came to the breakfast table with wet hair. He had just washed it.

"Why don't you use the hair dryer in my room?" I asked.

"When I use the hair dryer, it blows up my hair and I look as if I've put my finger in an electric socket," he said.

"It won't," I advised, "if you leave your hair a little damp, put the dryer on a cool setting for a few seconds, and then brush your hair."

See what I mean?

A father has to know these things if he hopes to raise a sturdy son who can cope in the modern world.

Junior doesn't want you to show him the secret of whittling a stick, or playing *My Old Kentucky Home* on a harmonica he bought for fifty cents at the corner store.

He couldn't care less that you have a terrific card trick that nobody can figure out.

So you can make a toy tank out of a thread spool, a match-stick and an ordinary elastic band?

Big deal.

What a son wants to know now is if he can get away with Springtime in the Rockies after-shave on a heavy date, or is Tahitian Musk definitely better for after-five wear?

Yes, yes, it's wonderful to know all the choruses to *Row, Row, Row Your Boat*, but what goes with a brown corduroy jacket, tan slacks, and an expensive floral-patterned Mr. Harold sports shirt? Pukka beads? A plain 10K gold chain with astrological sign pendant? Or is the basic silver rape whistle more fitting?

A father is supposed to have the answers to these difficult questions.

Can you fix a pocket calculator? Do you know a decent place to get hair styled for under seven dollars including shampoo? Will a headband make a person prematurely bald? Do you know how to advance a calendar watch?

Does medical research have anything significant to say about tight pants? What's the weather like during the March school break in Moscow? Will a beef bourgignon stain come out of a surplus German army combat shirt with water? How much would it cost to motorcycle across South America?

Believe me, playing father gets tougher every year.

Just a few days ago Stephen bought a blue dinner jacket with brocaded lapels from a discount clothing store for fourteen dollars, and they tossed in a dress shirt (with 1962 style collar) as a bonus.

The next day Stephen asked if it was too dressy to wear to Mr. Thornton's class, and if it would look right with his khaki pants—the ones held up by the leather belt with the World War I army buckle.

I said it would be fine but, between you and me, it was strictly a guess.

Until Stephen asks me something simple, like how to make a beanie out of an old fedora, I'm basically winging it as a father.


# A Date's Dad . . .

THANKS TO OUR JANE (WHO WILL BE SIXTEEN NEXT MONTH) I've assumed a new role in life, that of father of the date.

Of course it's strange to me but so far I've found out . . .

A father of the date, when a boy arrives at the front door, does not yell up the stairs, "You'd better move your cheeks. Dreamboat is here."

A father of the date does not bring out baby pictures.

A father of the date does not ask a boy to take off his shoes before he comes in, even if the mother of the date has just waxed the floors and is in the mood to kill at the first sign of dirt.

A father of the date does not make pimple jokes.

A father of the date does not ask a boy about his parents' marital status, his marks in math, if he's started to shave yet, or what kind of a career he has in mind for himself when he gets out of school and is able to support a family.

A father of the date does not tell stories about how tough things were when he was young, and how he had to get the date's mother home by 11:30 when they dated.

A father of the date does not straighten a boy's necktie on first meeting, or offer him a Kleenex for his pocket if he sniffs.

A father of the date does not armwrestle, attempt to lift said date over his head in a display of strength, or make pointed remarks about Donny Osmond being too young to marry.

A father of the date does not refuse to let the happy couple out of the house until they boy gives his word that the van parked out front is not his.

A father of the date does not notice braces on teeth.

A father of the date does not send the date's little brother into the front room every fifteen minutes to see what's going on.

A father of the date definitely does not ask a boy if he'd like to watch the Stanley Cup playoffs on TV with him rather than going out.

A father of the date does not let his knees buckle visibly when he learns which movies the boy wants to take his daughter to.

A father of the date does not say John Travolta stinks.

A father of the date does not mix up boyfriends and call them, gasp, by the wrong name.

A father of the date does not examine corsages for price tags.

A father of the date does not greet a boy while wearing a sweater with the elbows out, even if it is a favorite.

A father of the date does not make a big scene just because

the stereo is on full and the heavy furniture on the third floor is vibrating.

A father of the date does not peek out the front window for a better look.

A father of the date does not flick porch lights.

A father of the date does not holler down the stairs when it's just a little after midnight, "It's time your friend went home."

And, finally, a father of the date does not add, "After your friend has gone, let the dog out in the backyard for a whizz."

Being a father of the date is quite a challenge.

# Handling Teen Calls

THE OTHER EVENING THE TELEPHONE RANG AND A LOVELY female voice asked, "Is Stephen there?"

As it happened, our eldest wasn't, so I said, "I'm sorry, he's out."

I should have left it at that.

However, I broke the cardinal rule of being the father of a teenager while answering a telephone.

"Is that Debbie?" I asked.

Boom, crash and thud.

As soon as the words were out I knew I had made a terrible mistake.

"No," was the rather chilly reply. "It's . . ."

Of course it was a totally different name, the name of somebody who obviously didn't know Debbie even exists or, if she did, wasn't happy about it.

What a fool I am.

With three teenagers in the house, I should know you never mention a name over the phone and give away a son's (or daughter's) secrets.

You say, "Hello, there" or, "Hi, I'm sorry but you missed Stephen. Is there any message?" You can even say, "He's out but he won't be long."

But you don't cough up a free name and put your teenager in possible hot water with someone he's probably told is the only one in his life.

When will I learn?

I am pretty good now in that I never say, when a teenager at our house gets a call, "He (or she) is in the bathroom. I'll take a message."

Bathroom references are "gross."

Also, I never say, "He's over at Bill's. Maybe you can reach him there."

Giving away a teenager's social calendar is just as taboo as giving away a free name. You've got to be noncommittal. "Stephen will be sorry he missed you" is okay. Ditto, "Jane was talking about a movie, but she may have changed her mind," a statement that gives her lots of leeway and will not stand up in a court of law.

On the other hand, a teenager expects his or her father to pump as much information out of a caller as possible.

The absolute minimum is (a) who is calling, (b) the time of the call, (c) where the caller can be reached and (d) the sex of the caller.

You can forget about (a), (b) and (c), but heaven help if you flub (d).

Establishing the sex of the caller is absolutely vital and any father who misses out on that one is definitely in trouble. Unfortunately, when your teenagers have friends whose voices haven't changed yet, it isn't easy.

Other things a teenager expects a father to learn are:

Was the call (in your opinion) to invite said teenaged son or daughter to a party, school dance, etc., or did the caller sound like someone who only wanted the title of the book required for the French course."

As a guess (in the case of a call for a teenaged daughter) would you say the caller was probably six feet tall with a clear complexion?

Why do you think the caller didn't leave a number and, in your estimation, do you think he (or she) will call back if said teenager sits by the telephone for an hour or so?

The pressure of being the father of a teenager is enormous when the telephone rings and sometimes you just want to let it ring rather than risk making a mistake.

Fortunately, with teenagers in the house you know one thing: the call is never for you.

# Behind Times

OUR STEPHEN (WHO IS EIGHTEEN) CAME HOME FROM A disco the other evening with distressing news: while minding his own business on the dance floor, some girl he had never seen before reached over and pinched him on the bum.

According to the account we received, the assaulter was about twenty, had a dynamite figure and gave Stephen a cheeky grin when he turned in total surprise.

Fortunately, Stephen was with a date, so the whole sordid business went no further, but Stephen's mother and I were seething, of course.

Can a young lad no longer boogie in safety on the hardwood surfaces of this city? Must he keep his wits about him and his vitals protected even during the intricacies of The

Bump to make certain no lusting female, half-crazed by the sight of his plunging Pierre Cardin loungewear, takes unwanted liberties with his person?

For someone of my generation, it's totally unthinkable. Why, when I was Stephen's age, a male person could fox trot, waltz and dip to his heart's content in the school gymnasium without fear of being womanhandled every time he box-stepped past a dark corner.

In all my years of swinging and swaying with Sammy Kaye, not once did I have to ward off the impudent grope or the lecherous pat. Women respected men for their minds then, and understood when we told them we were "saving" ourselves for marriage.

No more apparently.

"Perhaps this young creature mistook you for somebody else," I suggested hopefully to my eldest. "Or else it was an accident."

"I don't think so," Stephen replied. "I think I can tell a deliberate pinch when I feel one, and she definitely smiled at me."

"You don't suppose she was in the middle of snapping her fingers to the music when your bottom happened to get in the way, do you?"

"No."

"Perhaps she works in a clothing store and was feeling the texture of your trousers. That's how they do it you know, between the fingers."

"She pinched more than cloth," Stephen insisted.

"This is even worse than I suspected," I said. "If you eliminate the music and the cloth, it means she was interested in only—my God! Thank heaven you were with somebody. If you had been alone, it's anyone's guess what might have happened to you."

Stephen shot back an answering nod to indicate he had, indeed, thought about the possibilities.

Unlike other males his age who might have wept and made their complexions blotchy after such a harrowing experience at the hands of a female stranger, Stephen remained composed, and I was proud of him.

"I don't want this one unfortunate incident to change your attitude toward women," I cautioned. "There are lots of them out there who can control their hands at a dance and not get out of line. However, as a precaution, I think you should take some preventative steps to avoid similar pawings in the future."

"Like what?" he asked.

"First, I'd buy trousers that are a size or two too big. You're just asking for trouble if you wear form-fitting ones in front of some sexually-liberated, twenty-year-old female who is only interested in a one-night stand.

"Next, for extra protection, put a thick hankie in the back pocket of the baggy trousers. Not only will it give you a lumpy appearance that should be as good as a cold shower to any female out for a good time, it will provide protection in the event she still tries to get fresh during a Barry Manilow number.

"Finally, try not to turn your back on a female if she is pawing the floor with one foot, has steam coming out of both nostrils and spits in her hands as she walks in your direction. She's obviously up to no good."

Stephen said he would weigh my words carefully because, "I don't think any one in the country knows more about turning off women than you do."

It was difficult holding back the tears. It's not often an eighteen-year-old son pays his father such a glowing tribute.


# No Toys for Dad

THE YEARS HAVE A NASTY WAY OF SNEAKING PAST AND IF I needed a further reminder all I have to do is look at the children's Christmas lists.

No longer do they painstakingly print out requests in inch-high crayoned letters to Santa at the North Pole asking for a "bingy" (Stephen's word for a toy xylophone he had his heart set on fifteen or sixteen years ago) or a doll that wets herself.

That day, alas, is long gone.

Stephen this year wants Santa to cough up the necessary for a Pro Drivers course and, as a stocking stuffer, insurance coverage for the heady hours when he slips behind the wheel of the family Chevelle and heads for the favorite disco with a lovely dish beside him.

Daughter Jane has opted for dance lessons—modern jazz stuff—and some knockout Danskin outfits that will cause spectators to tumble out of their balcony seats when she does her stuff.

Even Richard whom I counted on to ask for a Dinky toy car he could run across the living room carpet and say "brrrum, brrrum" on Christmas, yes even trusty Richard has requested grown-up stuff—a cord suit, Brut hair shampoo, a couple of neckties. He might just as well have plunged the knife all the way in and asked for a razor.

What has happened?

It seems only yesterday that Stephen was prepared to feed Dancer, Prancer, Vixen and Comet, too, if need be, for an entire year if dear old Kris would only leave a Big Bruiser truck under the holiday spruce.

He was just as nuts about getting a Man From U.N.C.L.E. gun, the one with the secret opening in the carrying case through which a clever lad could fire a plastic bullet at evil men bent on world conquest.

Jane never aimed higher than an Easybake oven, one which she could use to turn out hard cookies and brownies, eats no decent daddy would ever refuse even if it did mean sharp abdominal pains for the next 24 hours.

And Richard? Was he the one who promised to be good for the next thirty-seven years if only he could get a Secret Sam outfit and the wonderful Gunfight at the OK Corral set?

He was definitely enraptured by the Popeye punching bag that sat on the floor and was bigger than he was. How many flying leaps he took at that Christmas present I couldn't even guess, but 300,000 wouldn't be far out.

And now it's come down to driving lessons, dance outfits, and crummy neckties.

Of course I realize that by Christmas day they will be nineteen, sixteen and fourteen years of age.

But is that any reason to turn their backs on Silly String,

Leggo, Ready Ranger sets, Mr. Action, the immortal Johnny 7 kit, Hot Wheels and all the other items that set their hearts soaring in past Christmases?

If Stephen, Jane and Richard aren't interested themselves, they should at least consider Daddy.

What am I going to do on Christmas morning, play with Richard's new shirt or see if I can get Stephen's driving brochure to fly across the room?

I wonder if the missus would like a Darth Vadar helmet.

# Scoops

JACKIE AND I ARE ALONE IN THE HOUSE FOR THE FIRST time in nearly nineteen years, all three children being away on vacation, and it's made a tremendous difference in our lives.

Here are just a few things we've discovered:

You can kiss without anyone saying, "Cut that out."

You can turn on the radio and get the same station you had on when you turned it off, and not a blast of rock 'n' roll.

You can spend an evening at home and never hear the telephone. Ditto the front door bell.

Two bath towels can last an entire day.

You can serve liver and bacon (with onions) and not get a barrage of "Yuk!"

You can serve dinner AFTER 6:30, even as late as 6:35, and the world will not necessarily come to an end.

You can get something on TV besides *Laverne and Shirley, Monty Python,* and reruns of *Adam 12.*

A mother can try as hard as she wants but she cannot cook for two people and, if she makes chili, it will last anywhere from nine days to two weeks.

A quart of orange juice can be placed in the refrigerator at 4 o'clock and still be there at 6 o'clock, with no sticky spots on the kitchen floor.

A person can pick up the newspaper and find the comic section, even if the edition has been in the house for over sixty seconds.

Besides holding coats, books, wet bathing suits and bicycle parts, the chesterfield in the front room can be used to sit on.

The family dog can find ways to put in the day without having anyone blow up her nose with a straw or, during a deep sleep, shout "Bow Wow!" in her ear.

You can step into a bathroom without somebody bellowing, "How long will you be?"

You can get all your socks back washday.

A person can go twenty-four straight hours without having to say, "Don't you think you should have put a paper on the floor first?"

It is also possible to spend garbage night doing something other than scraping gum off the bottom of a wicker wastebasket with your fingernails.

You can sleep through an entire night without keeping one ear open to make certain everyone's in, and the front door double-bolted.

You can buy enough ketchup.

You can get yourself a treat at the market (black cherries, for example) and not be forced to hide it at the back of the refrigerator behind the broccoli.

A pair of jeans can fit on a clothes hanger as well as on the bedroom floor.

A dinner can be stretched out past six minutes.

A conversation can be held around the breakfast table without a single mention being made of driving lessons, and the absolute necessity of having same as a birthday present.

You can shop at the supermarket with $100 and not run short.

An adult can go twelve minutes without discussing somebody's complexion problems, and still not suffer any withdrawal pains.

There is such a thing in the world as leftover pie.

You can dress without going to somebody else's closet to retrieve your belongings.

Without too much effort, it is possible to balance on all

four feet of a kitchen chair.

Finally, we've discovered our stereo can be turned down.
Be still, my heart!

# A Farewell to Little Arms

OUR STEPHEN WAS INTRODUCED TO READERS OF THIS
journal on February 27, 1963. He was three years old then
and proud Papa was bursting out in paragraphs for the new
employer.

Stephen, I reported, liked to stand by the record player,
fiddle with knobs in best mad scientist fashion, and announce
to all within listening range, "I'm going to blow up the 'erf."

Whenever I had a cold, he'd reach to my lips, squeeze shut
his little fists, and assure Daddy, "I've got the germs." He'd
then throw them to the ground, and jump up and down,
presumably breaking their little necks.

When Stephen was somersaulting on the front room rug,
he was "upside down," when he was standing, he was "upside
up."

If he got mad, he didn't shout and holler. He merely stared into your face and said, "I'm giving you my eyebrows."

Why all the nostalgia now? Why the memories of a little boy who usually skipped five when he counted? Why the warm reflection of that day on a Florida beach when, after playing long enough in the ocean, Stephen asked his father to "pull the plug" and make the water go away?

Well, Stephen is eighteen now and leaving for Europe on his first big adventure. He'll be gone most of the summer, touring Britain, Holland, Belgium, France, Austria, Germany, Italy, Switzerland.

He has a Youth Hostel card, a Eurail pass, money saved up from his job this past year at the supermarket, a passport, the addresses of a few friends.

Yes, he's well prepared.

But somehow old Dad still hates to let go. For heaven's sake, it was only a twinkling of an eye ago that we let him out of the house with a piece of paper pinned to his coat that said, "Please leave me outside!" so he wouldn't talk his way into a neighbor's for a cookie.

And now he's off to see the world, a young man now, with no message pinned to his shirt but all kinds of hope under it.

He's finished high school where he and a friend started a newspaper and acted as its editors-columnists-business-managers-typists-layout men and chief worriers.

He's been on television as a member of the school's *Reach For The Top* team; he was in a musical at the old high school, on the chess team, and he and some friends have just made a mini-movie based on a skit he helped write.

Next September he'll be at university and . . .

I remember when Stephen used to hold up old popsicle sticks and conduct "interviews" with Fat Stuff (his sister Jane who was only one at the time, and not exactly a glib talker).

I remember his first birthday party when, with his usual sense of the dramatic, he took his first steps and crossed our gray rug without a helping hand.

Now it's an ocean he's crossing and there will be thousands of moments in the weeks ahead when I'll wonder where he is, and if he's all right.

Of course he will be. He's a fine person, bright, kind, and a joy to have around the kitchen table at the end of a day.

Still, there'll be mornings when I'll look at the office telephone and wonder why it doesn't ring and a cheery voice ask, "Would you like company for lunch, Dad?"

Dad always does.